Telling God's Story

Year Four Activity Book: The Story of God's People Continues

Student Guide and Activity Pages

Edited by Justin Moore

With Activities and Illustrations by
Kevin Boston, Earnest Graham, Justin Moore, Jessica Otto, Shelby Otto,
Colleen Sharpe, and Jeff West

Olive Branch Books
Charles City, Virginia

This book is to be used in conjunction with *Telling God's Story, Year Four Instructor Text and Teaching Guide*; ISBN 978-1-945841-30-9 (available as a PDF from Well-Trained Mind Press)
OR
ISBN 978-1-945841-31-6 (available as an e-book wherever e-books are sold).

Table of Contents

Using This Student Guide

This Student Guide is designed to accompany *Telling God's Story: Year Four Instructor Text and Teaching Guide,* by Rachel Marie Stone (available on PDF or e-book). It expands on the lessons in that book, providing coloring pages, projects, games, and memory work. Some of these activities provide opportunities to put the lessons into practice; others help the student review the content presented in the lesson; still others reveal the ways in which artists in different eras have depicted biblical stories. For each lesson in the *Instructor Text,* this *Student Guide* contains at least one activity and a coloring page.

A Typical Week in This Curriculum

Aim to complete one lesson per week. Each lesson in the *Instructor Text* opens with a brief word of explanation to the parent; this will help you in helping your children process the content of the lessons. You should spend a few moments reading the parent section ("What the Parent Should Know") from the *Instructor Text* the night before the lesson so you can ponder a bit; or if you prefer, read it right before the lesson so it is fresh in your mind—whatever works for you. The important thing is that you spend some time becoming familiar with the information so you can be of more help to your children. The purpose of these parent sections is to orient you to the biblical passage for that day. The parent sections are more detailed and complex than the scripted lessons; this will give you a broader handle on the issues surrounding the passage. It will also give you a greater vantage point from which to look at the lesson itself and, perhaps, to address questions that might come up.

Next, you may wish to read the scripted lesson from the *Instructor Text* to the student on the first day as he or she colors the coloring page for that lesson in the *Activity Book,* and then to complete projects on another day. Alternately, you may read the scripted lesson on the first day, complete the coloring page on the second, and complete the project or activity on the third.

In a group setting that meets once a week, plan to read the scripted lesson as the students color and then to conclude the day's study with the game or project.

Photocopying and Distribution Policy

For families: you may make as many photocopies of the student pages as you need for use WITHIN YOUR OWN FAMILY ONLY. Photocopying the pages so that the book can then be resold is a violation of copyright.

Schools, co-ops, and churches MAY NOT PHOTOCOPY any portion of this Activity Guide. You may purchase a classroom license ($100 per volume, per year) that allows duplication for school, church, and co-op use. For more information, please contact our parent company, Well-Trained Mind Press: email support@welltrainedmind.com or call 1.877.322.3445.

Unit 1

Jesus Departs—And God is Faithful

Lesson 1: Continuing Jesus' Story

Review Activity

Word Search: Witnessing Jesus's Life and Actions

Materials

- Witnessing Jesus's Life and Actions Word Search (Page 4)
- Pencil

Directions

1 Tear out Student Page 4, the "Witnessing Jesus's Life and Actions" Word Search.
2 Tell the student, "You use your five senses of sight, hearing, touch, smell, and taste to learn about the world around you. As you learn about Jesus's life and actions here on earth with his followers, imagine using your senses to try to figure out what was happening. Then imagine telling others about what your senses told you."
3 If the student needs help, give them hints using the answer key below.

E	Y	E	W	I	T	N	E	S	S			L	L	E	M	S
	S			E	E		N	X			N				C	
		N	T		S	E			A		O			E		
A		S	E		T	P				M	T		N		E	
T	A			S	I		E				I	T		L		N
T			I		M			C			C	N	B			O
E		L			O				T		E	I	E			I
N	S				N	T				A	G			R		T
T	O	U	C	H	Y	N				N	T			O	E	A
I	U					A			A			O		V		V
V	N					R	E	T	R	O	P	E	R	A		R
E	D		P	U	N	G	E	N	T			E		L		E
						A					S	N	I	F	F	S
W	A	T	C	H		R				B						B
T	N	A	M	R	O	F	N	I	O							O

Coloring Page

The Next Chapter of Jesus' Story

The book of Acts is "Volume Two" of the story about Jesus begun in the Gospel according to Luke. This second book tells of how Jesus helped his followers continue his work. They told people what they had learned and seen about him, and they showed how he had changed their lives and behavior.

Witnessing Jesus's Life and Actions Word Search

Find and circle these words. The words can be vertical, horizontal, or diagonal. They may be written forward or backward.

Nouns:		Verbs:		Adjectives:
informant	testimony	observe	touch	attentive
spectator	observation	watch	smell	tangible
eyewitness	sound	examine	sniff	fragrant
sense	scent	notice	taste	pungent
reporter	flavor	listen		

E Y E W I T N E S S I P L L E M S
S S J I E E L N X I V N U W P C O
K I N T R S E N Y A R O A M E J M
A Q S E F T P R H A M T V N T E I
T A V H S I X E I P L I T O L N N
T D Y I Y M O J C J U C N B Q K O
E Z L E K O T I K T I E I E U S I
N S P O A N T A D E A G W Y R A T
T O U C H Y N V U W N T T E O E A
I U K P C B A Q Y A L E O U V Z V
V N Q S Z U R E T R O P E R A H R
E D S P U N G E N T B X E D L L E
I P A T B R A O F M C S N I F F S
W A T C H C R O C F B I N G D I B
T N A M R O F N I O L E A M A G O

Luke & Acts
Two Parts of the Same Story

Lesson 2: Gone But *Not* Gone

Group Game

Taking Up Jesus's Mission

Materials

- buckets, shovels, plastic piping, toy medical and dental tools, medical/dental supplies such as bandages, stuffed farm animals, toy eggs, milk cartons, seed packets, spades, ziploc bags of soil, pencils, paper, math manipulatives, chalkboard/whiteboard, chalk/markers, books, pots, food, serving spoons, play money, and anything else you wish to add as imagination-provoking props!

Directions

1. Say to the students, "Today we are going to improvise [explain that term if necessary] short skits about taking up Jesus' mantle. In small groups, you'll have fifteen minutes to invent a skit that solves a problem that I will give to each group. You can decide if there will be talking or if it will be silent. You can choose to use props. Then each group will perform the skit for the rest of us."
2. Divide the students into groups of two or three each. Give each group a problem for them to act out a solution to. Read carefully and slowly to them, "Imagine that we are picking up Jesus' mantle (coat or robe) as he is taken to heaven; in the same way that Elisha picked up Elijah's mantle as Elijah was being taken to heaven, and carried on Elijah's work. Then think about what Jesus taught—how might he have handled the problem I'm giving you? As you figure out how to live out what Jesus taught, you are carrying on his work, or, 'taking up his mantle!'" Send each group to a space where they can work. Put the props in a central location so they can pick out what they need as they come up with ideas.
3. Check on the groups to help if they get stuck in improvising.
4. Give a five-minute warning before it's time for everyone to come back together for the performances.
5. Give each group a turn on the staging area to act out their skit. Before each group starts, read aloud the problem each group is acting out a solution to.

Problems (feel free to add to this list, adapt problems, or add specific scenarios if you think your students need more concrete ideas):

- A community needs clean water and sanitation.
- A town needs help cleaning up after a natural disaster.
- A person needs urgent medical and/or dental care and can't afford a doctor or a dentist.
- A family needs a few farm animals to provide milk and eggs.
- A neighborhood needs seeds, tools, and soil for making and maintaining a food garden together.
- A child who isn't in school for some reason needs help in reading, writing, and arithmetic skills.
- A young adult living in a shelter needs help in learning to obtain food, cook, and handle money.
- A person who has difficulty being around people wants to learn how to get along with people.

Option 1
Give all the groups the same problem to solve, and observe the differences in how each group interprets a solution.

Option 2
Provide big rectangles of paper or cloth (such as old sheets) to use as mantles. Let each group pick up a "mantle" before they get to work on their skit. They may even figure out a way to incorporate the mantle into the skit! You could even place the mantle across their shoulders as they go off to work.

Coloring Page

Jesus Says Goodbye

Jesus says goodbye to his disciples but promises that he will always be with them, through his Spirit.

Acts 1:9-14
Jesus' Friends Will Continue His Work

Lesson 3: What is an Apostle?

Group Game

Journey With Good News

Materials

- hard-boiled eggs—one for each student
- soup spoons—one for each student
- washable fine-tipped marker
- Good News message to write on each egg ("Jesus is alive again!" "We can have peace!" "We can be joyful!" "We can learn how to love each other!" etc.)
- playground with safe equipment, OR
- objects to create an obstacle course: chairs, string, chalk and pavement, hoola hoops, bean-bags, baskets or buckets, and anything else you have that will create some type of obstacle each student has to overcome during the journey . . . OR . . .
- an internet search for obstacle course ideas for kids—this site has twenty-five creative ideas: https://playtivities.com/obstacle-courses-for-kids/

Directions

1. In advance with the marker, write a Good News message on each egg.
2. Set up the obstacle course in advance. You can create your own, or you can use a local playground and map out the order of activities on the equipment. Make sure the activities can be carried out without the use of one hand.
3. Gather students and tell them, "We learned that an apostle is someone sent out to deliver a special and important message. Today we are going to experience being apostles. Each of you will have an egg on which a message is written. It will be your job to deliver that message, while carrying it on a soup spoon, to another person. You will make your way through an obstacle course, only this obstacle course is not like others—you are not to race through it, because you aren't being timed and you aren't competing with anyone. You should take your time so that you can keep your egg on your spoon. If you drop the egg; simply pick it up, put it back into the spoon, and then carry on through the course. Navigate each obstacle as well as you can while holding the egg on the spoon. When you get to the person at the end of the course, read the message on the egg to the person and hand them the egg."

4. Explain the course route to the students.
5. Position someone to receive messages at the end of the course.
6. Hand out the eggs and spoons, and let each student navigate the course. You can let students start the course a few seconds after each other, or you can let them complete the course one at a time. The important ideas are that it's not a race, they have to carry the egg on the spoon, and they have to read the message to the receiver at the end and give them the egg.
7. When everyone has completed the course, tell them, "The challenge of carrying an egg on a spoon while navigating the course somewhat shows us what it might have been like being an apostle. The twelve apostles didn't have the internet through which to send good news instantly! So they had to travel at what seems to us slow paces and long journeys to deliver good news. But the purpose of that job was joyful to them, as you may have seen when (receiver name) received your Good News!"
8. Wash the messages off the shells and let everyone enjoy a snack of hard-boiled egg.

Coloring Page

Sharing the News

This girl is telling her friend about something exciting. The apostles were people who learned from Jesus and then were sent to tell others about him . . . to "spread the news." Like them, we can tell others about who Jesus is.

Acts 1
Sharing Exciting News

Lesson 4: God's Deliverance: Making Something Good from Something Bad

Craft

Looking for the Beauty

Materials

Note: This activity requires some lead time as well as time for the geode crystals to grow. For an at-home activity, it would just need to be set aside and left alone. For a classroom activity, it would be best to have a place where students can leave the projects until the next week's class. However, if that is not an option, the student can carefully transport the geode home and let it grow there.

- Optional: a geode to show the students or an image of one
- You may either use real eggs or plastic Easter-type eggs; the real eggs require more work!
- Glue (a traditional classroom glue is fine)
- Epsom salt
- Food coloring
- Empty egg cartons or muffin tins (enough to hold one geode per student)
- Boiling water
- Bowl and spoon/small ladle

Directions

1. Say to the students, "In today's lesson, we talked about a tricky idea to understand. Our lesson said: '. . . in the Joseph story, in Peter's sermon, and in other places in the Bible, we are told that God uses even those things that human beings intend for evil—things that *are* evil—for good.' Remember, we are not saying that we are *glad* that the bad things happened. We are saying that sometimes we can still find something beautiful inside of something that doesn't look beautiful or good on the outside."
2. Ask the students if they have heard of a geode. If you have one to show them, do so now. If not, a color image of one works just fine. Show them how the outside looks like a plain, ugly rock. But when you turn it over and see the inside, it is amazingly intricate and lovely.

3. Tell the students that this is an example of what we talked about in the lesson. On the outside, something can seem all bad or terrible (like a plain, ordinary rock), but when you look inside of it, you might find out that there is still something beautiful and valuable to see.
4. Now explain that you'll begin the process of making your own geodes. **The prep work, for a classroom situation, would include the following: Coat each eggshell half (if you are using plastic eggs) with glue and a light dusting of Epsom salts, and allow it to dry for several hours. Alternatively, if you are using the real eggs, you will need to carefully crack it open and leave only a half-eggshell. Then, rinse and dry it before applying the glue and Epsom. Allow either option to dry inside of an empty egg carton or muffin tin.**
5. Next, you'll need to boil the water and remove it from the heat (this should be handled by the teacher, not the students). You will then add the Epsom salts in this proportion: 1 cup water to ½ cup Epsom. Keep stirring and adding Epsom salts until the salts will not dissolve. Then you can add food coloring.
6. When the water is cool enough to handle, help the students pour the solution into the eggshells. At this point, you will set the projects aside to grow. They may need several days to form into crystals. You can use the toothpick to break up the solution if it is forming a solid layer on top.
7. Once the eggshells are filled, tell the students: "Every time you see your geode, I hope you remember that, when bad things happen, we can still look for the beauty. Just like our geodes, which take a few days or weeks to grow, it might take a long time to see the beauty, but we can keep looking for it."

Coloring Page

Joseph and His Brothers

Joseph's brothers had treated him very badly. When they found out that he was now in charge of the land of Egypt, they were afraid he would get revenge on them. But he forgave them and gave them food to feed their families. Joseph said that God had taken even the bad things they did and used them to make something good happen.

Acts 2:22-41
Something Good From Something Bad

Unit 2

The Holy Spirit

Lesson 5: Tongues of Flame

Art-Study Activity

Burning Bush and Pentecost

Directions

1 Choose either the painting or the mosaic depiction of Moses and the burning bush:
   - Marc Chagall's painting *Moses and the Burning Bush*, from *The Story of the Exodus*, 1966 https://images.masterworksfineart.com/chagall2766.jpg
   - Mosaic of Moses and the burning bush, National Shrine of the Immaculate Conception, Washington, D.C. http://sdbnews.blogspot.ca/2013/03/homily-for-3d-sunday-of-lent.html (the two candles and the cross in front of the mosaic are not part of the artwork—tell students to ignore these)

2 Then choose either the painting or the stained glass depiction of the tongues of fire at Pentecost:
   - Emil Nolde's *Pentecost*, 1909 http://www.thearttribune.com/spip.php?page=docbig&id_document=1331
   - Stained glass image of Pentecost, Ascension Episcopal Church, Houston, TX https://www.ascensionepiscopalchurch.org/stained-glass.html

3 Print color pictures of the art, or gather students around a computer so that everyone can see the artworks.

4 Say to the students, "We just heard descriptions of the burning bush and the tongues of fire. Now we'll look at artworks that show ideas of what the fires might have looked like! We'll talk about and compare the artworks, and you'll have a chance to figure out what you like."

5 Looking at the two chosen artworks one at a time, pick and choose from the following questions to get the students examining and discussing the art.
   - a What do you see in this artwork? (objects, colors, lines, shapes, patterns)
   - b What do you see the most of? (objects, colors, lines, shapes, patterns) The least of?
   - c What seems closer in the artwork? (objects, colors, lines, shapes, patterns) Further away?
   - d Point to the flames from the (burning bush or Holy Spirit).
   - e What do you notice about the (person's or people's) facial expressions? Posture?

f Pretend you are describing this artwork to someone who isn't here—what would you say?

g From the written story, what did the artist include in the art? What did he or she leave out?

h Which art captures your interest more? Can you explain why?

Option: Compare the two burning bush or two Pentecost artworks to each other. Add this to Question 5g: Did either artist put something in or leave something out that the other artist did not? Question 5h would become: Which depiction of (the burning bush or tongues of fire) captures your interest more? Can you explain why?

6 To wrap up, say, "Can you imagine being Moses in front of that bush? What do you think it was like for him? How about the people who had tongues of fire over their heads at Pentecost, with all the noise of different languages being spoken? And isn't it amazing that no one seemed to have gotten burned in either of these two events? Isn't it even more amazing that the presence of God is for everyone?"

Coloring Page

Pentecost

On the day of Pentecost, the Spirit of Jesus came to the disciples, both men and women. The Spirit appeared like fiery flames above them. Jesus had promised that the Spirit would give them power to do and say the things that Jesus would do and say. He says that we can have that same Spirit too.

Acts 2:1-21
Flames of the Holy Spirit

Lesson 6: Making All Things New

Put It Into Practice Activity

Sharing With Those in Need

Below is a general list of items commonly needed by various types of shelters. Helping sponsor these local organizations is a great way for students to learn about needs right around them. Look over the list, choose an option from below to act upon, and help your students gather items to contribute to some specific local needs. If possible (check with the shelter you decide to help), take the students with you when you deliver the items.

Option 1: Pick a local shelter, find out what their current specific needs are, and bring that list to the students. Brainstorm with them and make a new list of what they will actually collect to deliver to the shelter.

Option 2: With students, look at the list of commonly needed items at shelters. Brainstorm with them to figure out what they can contribute. Perhaps they have extras of these items at home or perhaps they will be able to easily obtain some of these items. Once a list of available items is made, find out which shelter(s) will be able to use most of what you have available to you. Collect what is available, and arrange to deliver to a shelter.

Homeless Shelters:

mittens
hats
scarves
shoes
socks
underwear
toothpaste
toothbrushes
soap
shampoo
deodorant
sunscreen
washcloths
pajamas
thermal underwear
blankets
sheets
pillows
pillowcases
zipped plastic bags
clear plastic bags
backpacks
bandages
bus tickets
juice boxes
granola bars
gift cards to local eateries
umbrellas
raincoats
hand/feet warmers
funding/coins for laundry service
laundry detergent

Soup Kitchens:

muffins
cookies
biscuits
rolls
other baked goods
sandwiches
pre-cooked/reheatable meals
sponges/dishcloths
dish soap
kitchen scrubbies
dish towels
plastic spoons/forks/knives
recyclable cups/plates/bowls
kitchen ladles/serving spoons

Family Shelters:

diapers
baby wipes
bottles
baby formula
sealed baby food
washcloths
baby cereals
receiving blankets
onesies
sleepers
children's books
children's clothing
hand towels
bath towels
pajamas
bandages

Coloring Page

A Man Healed

Peter, acting in Jesus' name, healed a man who had been unable to walk. The man began leaping for joy and praising God for what had happened.

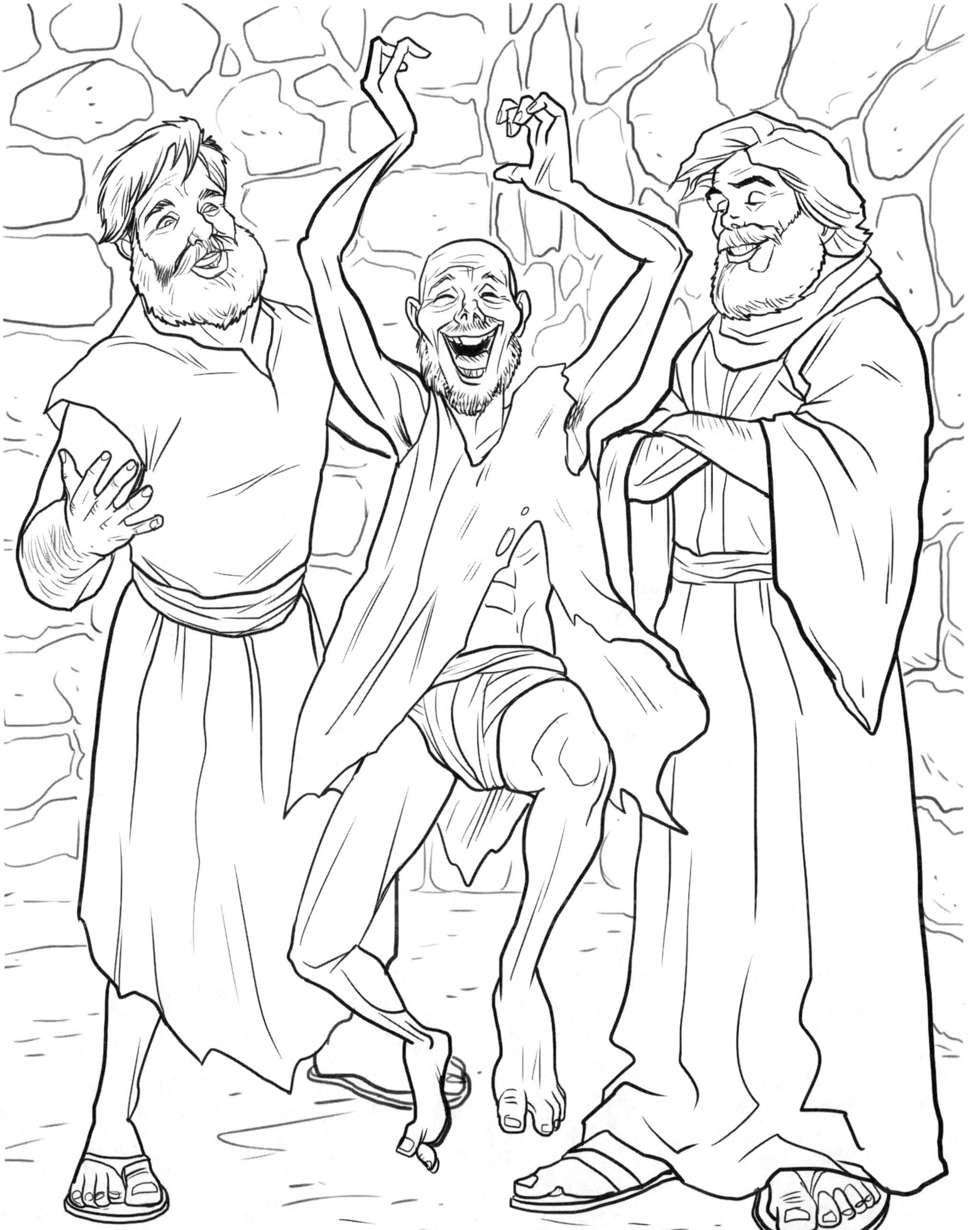

Acts 3
A Man Healed By the Power of Jesus

Lesson 7: Life in the Spirit

Group Game

The Game That Never Ends

For two or more players.

Materials

- "The Game That Never Ends" game board (Page 24) *Note: you may want to print extra copies of the board if you have more than four students.*
- A single die (one per game board)
- game place markers (candy pieces, coins, old game markers, or whatever is available)
- (optional for tolerant teachers) a YouTube video of "The Song That Never Ends" to learn the tune for the lyrics written below
- (optional for tolerant teachers) lyrics for "The Game That Never Ends"
- (optional for tolerant teachers) earplugs for those who won't want to hear humming (see Direction #2)

Lyrics (the lyric-writer apologizes in advance):

> This is the game that will not end;
> Yes, it goes on and on, my friend!
> Some kiddos started living it
> Like Holy Spirit does,
> And they'll continue living it forever just because
> (repeat)

Directions

1. Print out Page 24, containing the game board.
2. (optional) Using the tune from a YouTube clip, help the kids learn the song "The Game That Never Ends" so they can be humming it while playing the game.
3. (optional) Put in your earplugs if you don't want to hear the song on repeat!
4. Hand out game supplies (board, die, place markers)

5 Say to students, "Since we are now free to do good to one another, let's practice life in the Holy Spirit! The game will help us practice love, joy, peace, patience, kindness, faithfulness, and self-control."
6 Players take turns rolling the die and moving their marker forward the amount of spaces indicated by the die. Each player should then follow the instruction on the board square landed on. With fewer players for each game board, each player could spend a bit of time on an instruction.
7 Stop the game-playing (and the humming) when you want (you may want to give a five-minute warning).

Coloring Page

It's Not About the Rules

Sometimes when older children and younger children play games together, the older children become exasperated with the younger children because the younger children aren't following the rules. In the early days of the church, people often worried about needing to follow the rules that God had put down for his people long ago. Of course, many of Jesus' teachings were all about how following all the right rules isn't the way to God. Jesus himself is the way to God, and he showed us that the meaning and purpose of all of those rules is to love God and love other people, just as the point of rules in a game is to make the game interesting and fun.

The Game That Never Ends

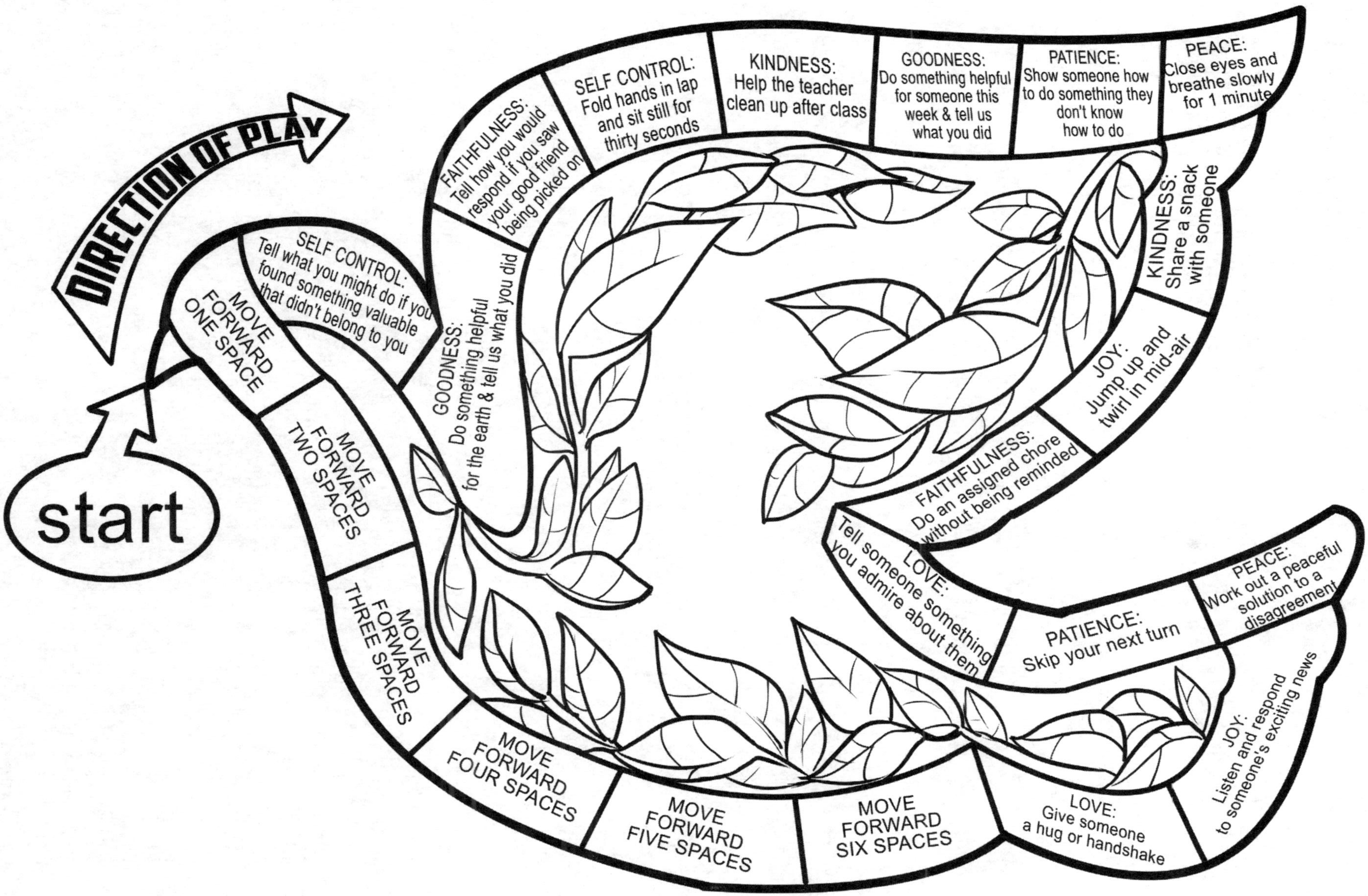

Galatians 5 & 6, Romans 8
Arguing Over the Rules

Unit 3

The Cost of Following Jesus

Lesson 8: Persecution by Religious Authorities

Review Activity

Becoming Brave

Materials

- "Becoming Brave" Crossword Puzzle (Page 24)
- Pencil

Directions

1 Tear out the "Becoming Brave" Crossword Puzzle (Page 29).
2 Say to the student: "Fill in the crossword puzzle by matching each word to its definition. Use one letter per space. These words describe qualities that Peter and John acquired through prayer and because Jesus's Spirit was helping them. They would need these qualities to deal with persecution. In our own lives, we, too, can ask God to develop these qualities in us. They are as useful and necessary today as they were two thousand years ago."
3 If the student needs help, refer to the answer grid below.

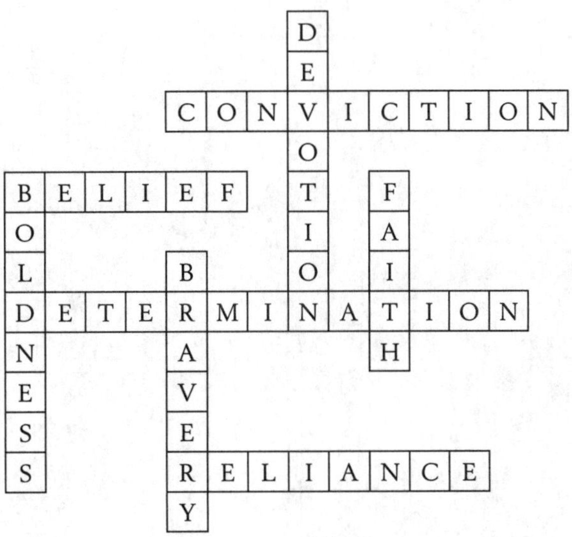

Coloring Page

Peter and John Get a Warning

The religious teachers didn't believe what Peter and John said about Jesus, and they thought Peter and John were uneducated and wrong. So they warned them not to teach anyone else about Jesus. But Peter and John didn't stop, because they had to do what God told them to do. God uses both educated and uneducated people to spread the news about Jesus.

"Becoming Brave" Crossword Puzzle

boldness	conviction	faith	devotion
reliance	belief	determination	bravery

Across:

2. A firmly held belief
3. Something one accepts as true or real
5. Having firmness or purpose
7. Dependence on or trust in someone or something

Down:

1. Giving time and resources to a person or an activity
3. Being willing to take risks
4. Complete trust or confidence in someone or something
6. Courageous behavior

Acts 4:1-31
The Religious Leaders Are Upset!

Lesson 9: Prison Doors Open

Craft

Make a Center of Gravity Toy

Materials

- tennis balls cut in half; one half for each student
- play-dough, clay, plasticine, or any other modeling compound that is child-safe and dense
- white paper
- scissors
- tape or glue stick
- crayons or markers to decorate the paper (don't use anything heavier such as stickers or glitter)
- Optional: plastic eggs (see Optional Take-Home Version at end of directions)

Directions

1. Put all the supplies out for students to use.
2. Say to the students, "Like the silly song about the cat in the lesson we heard today, this science demonstration is just a demonstration of the center of gravity and not a story about the Holy Spirit. However, the principle we will observe can remind us of the determination that Peter and John had in talking about Jesus."
3. Take a blob of compound—experiment with different volumes such as a fourth, a third, or a half of the volume of the half tennis ball. Roll the compound into a ball—the more tightly packed, the better.
4. Place the ball of compound in the center bottom of the half tennis ball and make sure it sticks.
5. Tap the cut edge of the tennis ball to see if it wobbles and then rights itself again. If it doesn't, adjust the volume of compound until it will do this. If there is interest and time, research the concept of a "center of gravity" and explain to students why the wobbling and uprighting is happening.
6. Create a paper tube whose openings are just slightly bigger than the circumference of the cut edge of the half tennis ball.
7. Tape one end of the tube to that cut edge. The tube can slightly overlap the side of the half tennis ball. Students may need help securing the tube to the ball.

8. Place the "toy" on a flat surface with the rounded part of the half tennis ball sitting on that surface. Lightly tap the side of the tube to tip the toy over.
9. If it doesn't right itself, start cutting off rings of paper from the tube, until the tube is short enough that the tipped-over toy will right itself. (Test it after each time you cut a ring off.)
10. Carry on with decorating the tube with markers and crayons and have fun playing with the center of gravity toy!
11. Remind the students: "The center of gravity in the dough ball inside the tennis ball is what is making the toy bounce back to where it came from, over and over again. Gravity also helps us to stick to the earth and not float off into space. One way to picture what is happening with Peter and John is to imagine that Jesus and the Holy Spirit are their center of gravity that helps them be brave and deal with their sufferings and keep coming back!"

Optional Take-Home Version: Instead of using half tennis balls, use large plastic eggs that open and that have rounded bottoms. The students can decorate the outside of the eggs with markers (permanent if you think your students will use them only on the eggs). After securing the dense dough in the bottom of the egg, have students replace the top of the egg. Thus they now have a center-of-gravity object that will demonstrate the principle.

Coloring Page

God Breaks Peter and John Out of Prison

Peter and John had been thrown into prison for teaching about Jesus. But when the guards came to get them for more questions, they were gone! God had broken open their chains and opened the doors for them to leave.

Acts 5:17-14

God Breaks Peter and John Out of Prison

Lesson 10: The Story of Stephen

Map Activity

The Christians Scatter

Materials

- One copy per student of the map page "The Christians Scatter" (Page 35)
- Crayons, markers, or colored pencils
- Completed map for students to copy from (Page 36—one copy per table, per student, or per group of students)

Directions

1 Make sure each student has a copy of the blank map "The Christians Scatter."
2 Tell the students they'll be copying features of the filled-in map to their own copy of the blank map. Let them know that this is the region of Jerusalem, Judea, and Samaria back in the time of Stephen, when the Christians had to flee from Jerusalem to many different areas because they were being chased by the religious and political leaders; and that some of the physical features of the region would have affected how the people scattered.
3 Make sure they use the color code so that they can see each individual feature when their maps are completed.
4 After the students are finished coloring their maps, ask the following question for discussion: "Tell me about the features you copied to your map. How would features such as rivers, mountains, lakes, seas, or grasslands have made things easier or harder for the people who were scattering due to fear?"

Coloring Page

Helping Those in Need

The followers of Jesus shared their money and food with people who didn't have enough. They chose seven helpers, called "deacons," to make sure that everything was shared fairly. Stephen was one of these helpers.

Lesson 10: The Story of Stephen

The Christians Scatter

The Christians Scatter (Completed Map)

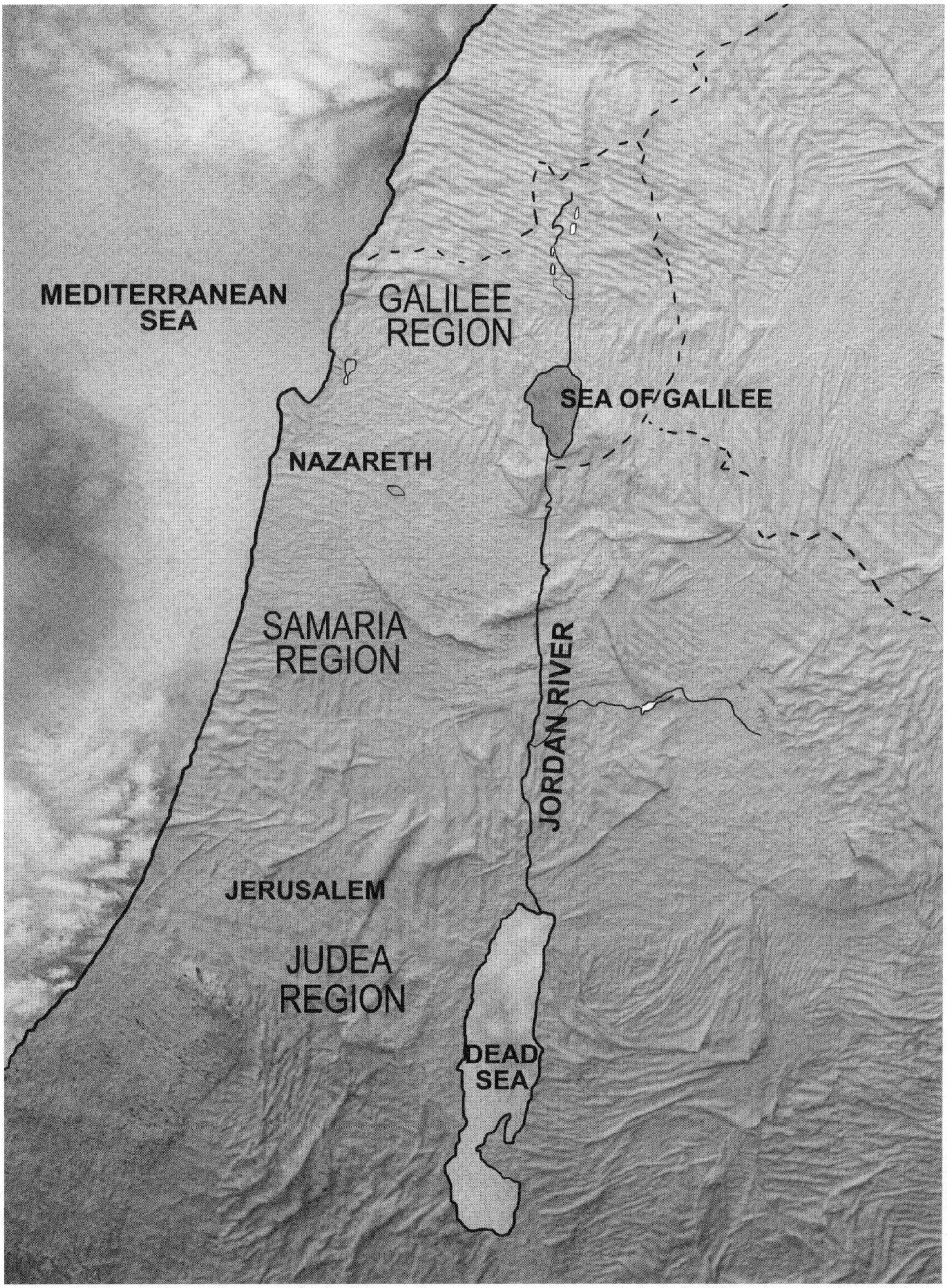

Acts 6:1-8:3
Helping Those in Need

Lesson 11: Setting Captives Free

Review Activity

Setting Captives Free

Here are three different options for reviewing the content of this week's lesson. Select the one that works best for your group.

Directions

Option 1:

1 Tell the students they are going to fill in an outline of what happened in Acts 16:16-40. They can answer in phrases or complete sentences, whichever you think is appropriate. The purpose is to reinforce to them the story they just heard read to them.
2 Give each student a pencil and a copy of "Complete the Outline: Setting Captives Free" (Page 41).
3 Tell them you will read questions to them to help them fill in the blank lines.
4 Referring to the Bible and the questions, read the questions and give all help needed with saying and writing answers. If you think it would be useful to your students to break a section down further (for example, section II C or III F), feel free to do that, too; using Arabic numerals.

Here are the questions to ask to help fill in the outline:

I. Actions of the slave girl and Paul
   A. What did she do under the influence of a spirit?
   B. How did that benefit her owners?
   C. What did she do to Paul and his companions?
   D. What did Paul do about that?

II. Consequences of Paul's actions
   A. What did the fortune-telling spirit do?
   B. What did the unhappy slave owners do to Paul and Silas?
   C. What did the magistrates command?

III. Overnight events

A. What were Paul and Silas doing in the prison while prisoners listened?
B. What happened to the prison during the earthquake?
C. What did the jailer try to do when he feared that the prisoners had escaped?
D. How did Paul prevent the jailer from harming himself?
E. How did Paul answer the jailer's question about saving himself?
F. What three things did the jailer then do?

IV. Daylight events
A. What did the magistrates command next?
B. What did Paul protest?
C. What did Paul challenge the magistrates to do?
D. What did the magistrates do and ask Paul and Silas to do?

Here is what the outline might look like after the questions are answered:

I. Actions of the slave girl and Paul
A. She predicted the future under influence of a spirit
B. She earned money for her owners by doing this
C. She followed Paul and his companions for days, shouting about who they were
D. Paul commanded the fortune-telling spirit to leave the slave girl

II. Consequences of Paul's actions
A. Spirit left the slave girl
B. Slave owners dragged Paul and Silas to face the authorities
C. Magistrates ordered for them to be stripped, flogged, and imprisoned

III. Overnight events
A. Paul and Silas prayed and sang hymns while other prisoners listened
B. Earthquake shook the prison, opened the prison doors, and loosened the prisoners' chains
C. Jailer tried to kill himself when he feared that prisoners had escaped
D. Paul reassured him they were still in there
E. Paul and Silas told him to believe in Jesus in order to be saved
F. Jailer washed their wounds, got himself and his family baptized, and fed them at his house

IV. Daylight events
A. Magistrates ordered for Paul and Silas to be released peacefully
B. Paul protested that they had been unfairly treated as Roman citizens
C. Paul challenged the magistrates themselves to escort him and Silas out
D. Alarmed magistrates escorted them and asked them to leave the city

Option 2:
An easier option for students or for bigger classes is to have them write a three- to five-sentence narration about the events in the story. Be sure the following elements are included:

- Paul rescued a fortune-telling slave girl from torment and got into trouble for this

- While Paul and Silas were praying in prison, an earthquake helped convince their jailer to follow God's ways
- Though authorities wanted Paul to leave prison peacefully, he protested and they were afraid

Option 3:
Have the students come up with a simple skit/play that tells the story of this week's lesson. Once they've practiced it, they can perform it for parents or friends.

Coloring Page

An Earthquake!

Paul and Silas were put in jail for teaching about Jesus. But an earthquake broke open their cell. The jailer was afraid that he would be killed for letting them get away. But Paul and Silas stayed and told him how to become a follower of Jesus.

Complete the Outline: Setting Captives Free

With your teacher's help, fill in the following outline of Acts 16:16-40.

I. Actions of the slave girl and Paul

  A.

  B.

  C.

  D.

II. Consequences of Paul's actions

  A.

  B.

  C.

III. Overnight events

  A.

  B.

  C.

  D.

  E.

  F.

IV. Daylight events

  A.

  B.

  C.

  D.

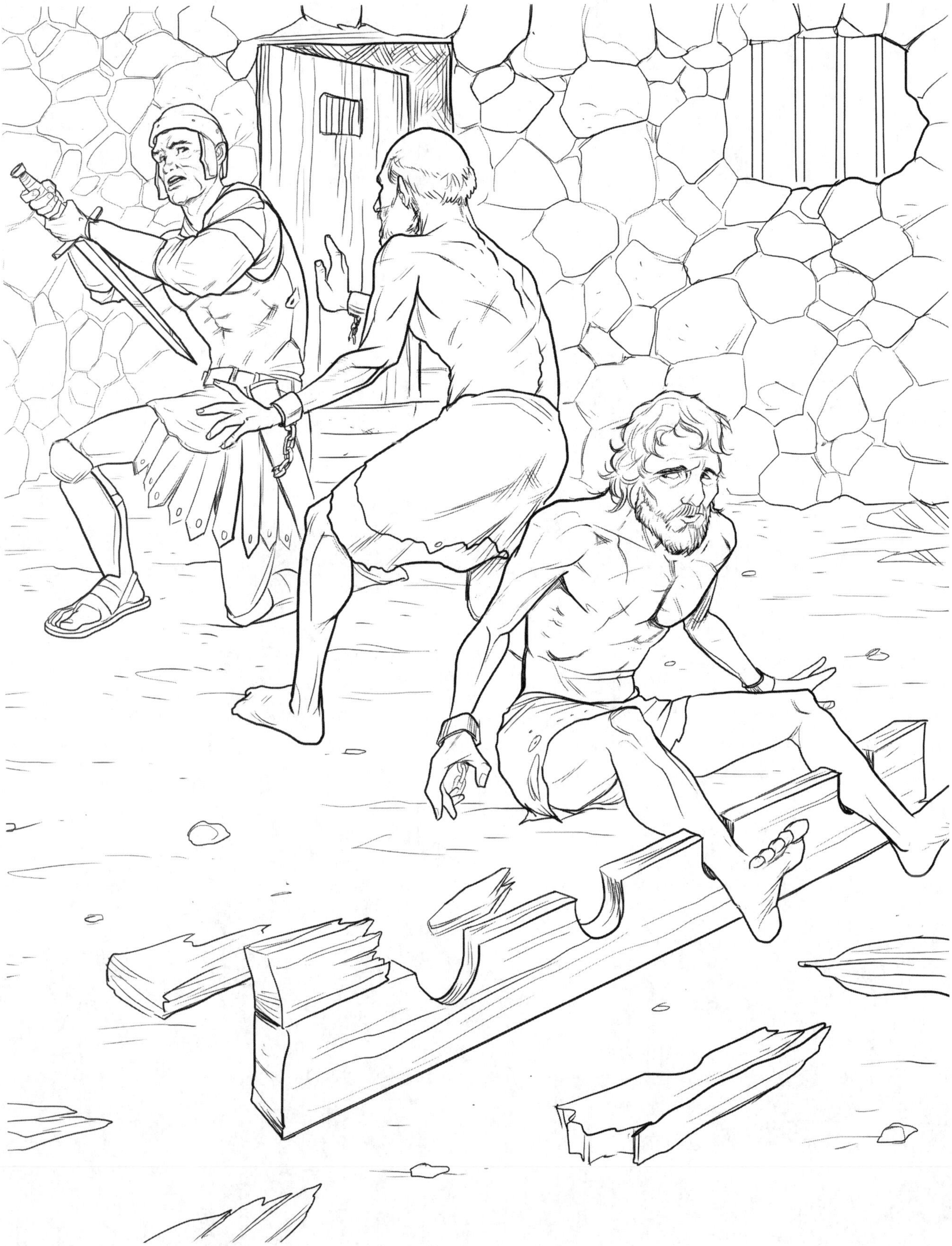

Acts 16:16-40
An Earthquake!

Lesson 12: How Can Trials Be a Joy?

Activity

Demonstration of Dispersion

Materials

- millet seeds (which are lightweight) or white rice (which is a bit heavier and might have a lesser visual impact of dispersion) or any colorable seed/grain that is affordable in your region
- different colors of liquid or gel food coloring (could use up to twelve, to represent the twelve tribes)
- spoons
- funnel—borrowed from a kitchen, or made by rolling a piece of paper into a cone and taping it closed
- containers (use the same number as the number of food colorants you will use)
- tarp, dropcloth, or pavement surface such as driveway or parking lot
- washable marker or chalk
- broom and dustpan
- 1/2 cup measure

Directions

Gather your students and assign the following tasks/steps as you see fit:

1. Place 1/2 cup of millet seeds into each container.
2. Add drops of one color of food coloring to the first container, and mix the food coloring into the millet seeds thoroughly with a spoon. Aim to get the whole batch uniform in its particular color.
3. Do the same with the millet seeds in each of the other containers, using a different food coloring and a different spoon for each container.
4. Spread the tarp or dropcloth in an open area that may get a bit messy, or go outside to the paved surface.
5. Using the marker or chalk, draw a target in the middle of the tarp/dropcloth/paved surface area being used. A big dot that everyone can easily see from a few feet away is sufficient.

6. With your arms straight out in front of you and parallel to the surface you are standing on, hold the funnel (narrow end facing down) directly above the target. Slowly pour the millet from the first container into the funnel. You may have to take a wide-legged stance so the seeds don't bounce off your legs in just one direction. Don't try to stop the seeds from scattering; just let them disperse.
7. Let everyone observe the dispersed seeds, and ask what they notice about distance, colors, and patterns.
8. Repeat Steps 6 and 7 with the seeds in the other containers, until all the millet has been dispersed.
9. Once all the millet has been dispersed, ask once more what they notice about the entire scene of seed dispersion. You can use their observations to reinforce the message of the lesson.
10. Use broom and dustpan to clean up the mess! Use the seeds to feed birds and explain that bird droppings will disperse the seeds even further than the funnel did.

Optional: You can use different sized funnels/funnel openings to change the rate and force at which the seeds fall to the target. You can also put seeds through the funnel at varying heights for the same purpose. The effects of dispersion will vary if you try these options.

Coloring Page

Spreading the Seeds Around

These birds take seeds from your yard and scatter them, helping plants grow all over. In much the same way, when people attacked the Christians and made them scatter, it didn't stop Jesus' message; instead, it spread it all over!

James 1
Spreading Seeds Around

Unit 4

Being a New Creation in Christ

Lesson 13: An Outsider is Welcomed In

Put It Into Practice Activity

Showing Hospitality--All Are Welcome in God's Family

Materials

- a warm sheltered meeting area, inside or outside depending on weather
- finger foods such as veggies/fruit, dip, cheese and crackers, muffins, cookies, etc.
- drinks: cold water, herbal tea, lemonade, hot chocolate, etc.
- trays or serving plates
- small plates, cups/glasses/mugs, spoons
- napkins: paper or cloth
- any decorative touches such as a tablecloth or a vase of flowers
- chairs or cushions for seating
- table (low or high, depending on seating available)
- list of possible topics of conversation

Directions

1. Select a person or group of people and invite them to visit your students. This person or group does not have to come to the group to share something or speak to the group; they simply come to visit. You can assure them that there is no agenda for the visit, except pleasant companionship. Put some care into whom you invite; you want someone who is somehow different from your group of students, but you don't want them to feel like a short-term project or a token friend; and you want to establish trust and friendship. You might share that your students are learning to give hospitality; that way, the invitees can decide whether or not they want to come.
2. On visit day before the guest(s) arrive, say to the students, "We learned through the story about Philip and the Ethiopian man that God welcomes everyone, no matter any differences. Today we will be welcoming (name of person or people) for a visit, so we will now prepare for their comfort and conversation with us! We'll need food and drink for refreshment, a warm and sheltered place to sit for comfort, and some ideas of things to talk about with our guest(s)."
3. After everyone's hands are washed, assign jobs for the students to do. This could be arranging food on trays, covering the table with a cloth, arranging trays and dishes on

the table, setting out napkins and decorative items, and arranging the seating around the table.

4 Explain to the students that they will be putting the guest first in everything, from choice of seat to choice of food and drink to choice in conversation.
5 When the guest arrives, have students show him/her to the seating area and invite him/her to sit with everyone around the table. Remind students to offer the food and drink to the guest before they offer it to anyone else.
6 Begin conversation by choosing a topic to ask the guest about.
7 At the end of your time together, have students thank the guest for coming and walk with him/her to the door.

Possible Topics For Conversation (feel free to add or subtract from this list—adapt it to your situation):

- favorite memory/books/music/art/movies
- closest family and friends
- hobbies or skills they enjoy practicing
- dreams/hopes/wishes for the future

Additional Options:
Write a short welcome speech for someone to read aloud! Or prepare a short welcome ceremony, such as a dance, a song, or a poetry reading. Or have each student start a new conversation topic from your list.

Coloring Page

God Welcomes All People

God's Spirit took Philip to meet a man from far away, so Philip could tell him the good news that God welcomes everyone.

Acts 8:26-40
God Welcomes All People

Lesson 14: Being a New Creation in Christ

Craft

New Creations Weavings

Say to the students, "As we read in the lesson, Jesus made it possible for us to live as new creations. Let's do a weaving project that can show us a little bit of what this means. We are going to use materials that are supposedly no longer useful to us to make a new and beautiful creation. Think of an old t-shirt that you don't want to wear anymore because the collar is frayed and stringy. What about a favorite pair of colorful socks that now have holes in them? Or plastic grocery bags, newspapers, and magazines we no longer need for their original purpose? As we do this project, let's look for what might look interesting in these weaving materials and use that in the final design. Even gray plastic bags have a shine to them! As you weave, think of someone to whom you'd like to give the final circular weaving as a decorative ornament. This is sort of like us becoming a new creation and showing kindness. God made us beautiful and useful, and he keeps making something beautiful out of us even though we make mistakes."

Note: The challenge here is to use all recycled materials (for example, don't buy new string) to demonstrate the idea of transformation from old to new. Also, feel free to make and warp the cardboard looms before class if you wish to save class time for the creative part of weaving. Steps 1 to 8 are detailed, but once you understand them, it won't take long to make up several looms. The students should at least do the weaving, though. You can prepare the weft materials in advance or let the students cut them as they please during class.

Materials

- corrugated cardboard (one 12" x 12" piece for each student)
- circular lunch plate and dinner plate (7-inch and 10-inch diameters)
- flexible tape measure for measuring and marking around a circumference
- pencil
- scissors
- tape

- strong string or twine, leftover from a project OR narrow strips of recycled non-stretch fabric (cotton, silk, and linen are stable choices—these will be used for warp threads)
- weft threads (see Options)

Option 1: colorful, patterned fabric from worn-out but clean clothing: t-shirts, socks, etc.
Option 2: colorful plastic grocery bags and polyethylene mailing envelopes (used but clean)
Option 3: colorful patterned papers from newspapers, magazines, or any other used, clean paper source

Directions

1. Using either the lunch or the dinner plate as a template, put the plate face-down on the cardboard and draw a circle on the cardboard.
2. Cut out the circle. This will be the cardboard loom.
3. Around the circumference of the circle, mark an **odd number** of evenly-spaced slits; then cut these slits in from the edge about a half inch. Spacing these slits roughly an inch apart, the 7-inch plate will yield about 21 slits and the 10-inch plate about 31 slits. You can choose to do more or less, as long as it is an **odd number** and they are fairly evenly spaced apart. If the weaving materials you will use are wide or thick, you will probably want to have a smaller amount of slits so there is more space between warp threads, especially towards the center, for weaving. These slits will hold the warp threads in place while the weft gets woven in.
4. Using the string, twine, or thin strips of non-stretch fabric (that is, the warp threads), begin to set up the warp on the loom. Tape an end of warp thread to the back of the loom.
5. Bring the thread through a slit to the front of the loom.
6. Cross the center of the loom with it, and bring it to the back through the slit opposite.
7. Look at the back of the loom. Through the slit to the right (or left, but be consistent) of the slit you just used, bring the thread to the front of the loom again.
8. Repeat Steps 7 and 8 until all the slits are used. After the thread is brought to the front of the loom through the final slit, bring the thread to the center of the "spokes" that have formed. Leaving a tail a few inches long, cut the thread. Use the tail to tie that last spoke to the central crossing of strings. A simple knot will do. The tail left will be tied to the beginning weft materials later. The warp should look like radiating spokes of a wheel and the number of spokes should be odd.
9. The materials in your option should be cut or torn into strips. These strips can be as wide or narrow as you want. Wide strips means fewer rounds of weft thread; narrow strips means more rounds of weft thread (and more chance of beautiful pattern and color in the overall woven design). Be mindful of the material; for example, if you use thin paper strips, they could tear. With wider strips of paper, you have the option of pushing them down the warp to make them look narrower, without the risk of tearing. Alternatively, you can twist strips of thin paper to make them stronger.
10. Take the first strip and tie it to the tail left in Step 8. The knot for this should be as close to the center as possible.
11. Take the weaving end of the weft strip and thread it over the warp spoke nearest the knot. Thread it under the next spoke. Go around and around like this, over and under, and always in the same direction (clockwise or counter-clockwise, but be consistent).

12 As you go around, use your fingers to push the threaded weft threads towards the center.
13 When you run out of weft strip or you want to change weft strips to add design variety, tie or tape the next one to the previous and continue weaving.
14 If you look at one spoke, you should see a pattern of "over, under, over, under" of weft thread up the length of the warp spoke.
15 When you have woven in all the weft threads you want and are satisfied with the design, tie the weaving end of the weft thread to the nearest warp spoke. Cut the thread, leaving a tail. Tuck that tail and it's knot between the weaving and the cardboard.

Coloring Page

A New Baby

In so many ways, we may seem to be exactly the same people we always were, even after we start to follow Jesus. We are not "born again" like a brand-new baby, but we are "born again" and "new creations" because our way of being in the world has changed. What we love and what we do has changed. Instead of living selfishly, worried mostly about our own things, when we follow Jesus, we leave behind those things and live as members of the new world that God is already making: a world of peacefulness, sharing, kindness, and fairness.

II Corinthians 5, I Peter 1
A New Baby

Unit 5

Who Is Paul?

Lesson 15: From an Enemy to a Brother

Activity

Saul's Transformation

Materials

- A copy of "The A-Maze-ing Transformation of Saul (Page 56)" for each student
- Pencils

Directions

1 Give each student a copy of Page 56.
2 Tell them, ""Through the maze, follow Saul's journey of transformation! Find your way to each stop in his journey."
   - Saul travels toward Damascus on a mission from the high priest
   - Bright light, Saul's blinding, and Jesus' voice
   - Arrival at Damascus while blind
   - Ananias comes and meets Saul and calls him "brother"
   - Saul's eyesight is restored and his name is changed

Coloring Page

The Road to Damascus

Saul was trying to throw Christians in prison, but Jesus appeared to him and showed Saul that he was real, and alive. Saul was transformed into Paul . . . no longer an enemy of Jesus, he would now spend his life telling people about how amazing Jesus is.

The A-Maze-ing Transformation of Saul

Acts 9:1-9
Jesus Confronts Saul

Lesson 16: What Paul Gave Up

Review

Paul's Transformation Word Scramble

Materials

- Paul's Transformation Word Scramble (Page 60)
- Pencils (one for each student)

Directions

1. Give each student a copy of Page 60 with the Paul's Transformation Word Scramble.
2. Say, "Unscramble the letters below to make words that describe Paul before he became a Jesus-follower and apostle."
3. If the students get stuck, help them with the hints below.
4. When the words are all unscrambled, have the students take the letters that the worksheet describes in order to find a new word, one that tells who was responsible for changing Paul.

Hints to give students if they get stuck:

- when a person judges
- when a person is tied to rules
- what group Paul belonged to
- when a person is boastful
- when a person strictly follows a particular religion

Answers:
judgemental
rulebound
Pharisee
proud
religious

Final answer: Jesus

Coloring Page

Paul Writes a Letter to a Church

Paul wrote many letters to the churches he helped to start, reminding them of what they had learned and about how to live as followers of Jesus. Some of these letters are in your Bible now!

Paul's Transformation Word Scramble

Unscramble the letters below to make words that describe Paul before he became a Jesus-follower and apostle.

natludgejem _ _ _ _ _ _ _ _ _ _ _

brudouenl _ _ _ _ _ _ _ _ _

sphireea _ _ _ _ _ _ _ _

druop _ _ _ _ _

gioriluse _ _ _ _ _ _ _ _ _

Now, take the following letters from the unscrambled words and put those into the blanks below to find out how Paul changed his ways!

- first letter
- fourth letter
- sixth letter
- fourth letter
- last letter

_ _ _ _ _

Philippians 3
Paul Writes a Letter to New Christians

Lesson 17: Paul, the Idols, and the Philosophers

Review

Characteristics of Jesus: What Heroes Embody These?

Directions

1. Begin by saying, "In the lesson, Paul saw many idols and statues to gods in the city of Athens. Now, heroes aren't exactly idols because they usually aren't made from materials such as clay or stone or wood or gold. But in our world today, we humans tend to admire and care about various heroes somewhat like the Athenians worshiped idols. We may have heroes from fictional books, poetry, sports, movies, television shows, musical bands, history, video games, or real-life family or friends. Some of our heroes might even be what many would consider "bad," such as Sauron, Darth Vader, the White Witch, the Grinch, or the Big Bad Wolf! Let's each think of a real or fictional hero we admire, and consider what characteristics of Jesus that this hero might have."
2. Let each student volunteer the name of a hero (yes, even villains). Using the list of characteristics that Jesus had, ask the student(s) which characteristics the hero had or has, and to give an example of why the student thinks the hero has this trait. You might ask, "What did (hero) do that shows this? What did (he/she) say that show this?" You could also ask, "How does that tell us about Jesus and God's love for us? What did Jesus do that shows this same characteristic?"
3. Give as much or as little time to discussing characteristics of each hero as you see fit, depending on number of students, time, interest, and depth of discussion.
4. When you think no one else has something to contribute, wrap up with, "Let's try to recognize, in our everyday lives, the characteristics of Jesus in people we meet with and in situations we encounter. If we practice doing this, we can more easily talk about Jesus and his ways with others."

Characteristics of Jesus (feel free to add to this list)

loving
compassionate
kind
fierce
strong
secure
faithful
joyous
friendly
servant
thankful

wise
confident
content
generous
dependable
creative
determined
loyal
selfless
honest
just

committed
forgiving
prayerful
humble
patient
self-controlled
gentle
righteous
approachable
giving
fair

Coloring Page

Paul In Athens

Paul was in Athens, a city in Greece, a place that was full of statues of gods. He told the people there about the one real God.

Acts 17
Paul In Athens

Unit 6

The Good News is for Everyone!

Lesson 18: Peter Goes to Cornelius' House

Demonstration

The Good News Is For All Of Us

Materials

- 1 clear glass or plastic container, 1 quart capacity
- 1 clear glass or plastic container, 1 cup capacity
- 1 clear glass or plastic container, 2 cup capacity
- ½ cup vegetable oil
- Food coloring
- ½ teaspoon salt

Directions

1. Say to the students, "In this lesson, we learned that the Gospel was for everyone, not just for one group of people. Our lesson said: 'Instead of people being kept separate from each other based on what they eat or don't eat, or who their parents were, or where they were born, the Holy Spirit is forming a new group: one that is formed when people believe in Jesus.' In this activity, let's show what happens when we let differences keep us apart, instead of together."
2. Set out a clear glass or plastic container able to hold at least one quart of liquid. Have a student add approximately ½ cup vegetable oil to the container. Then, using another clear jar or container, have a student add ½ cup water to that container. Add a few drops of food coloring to the water.
3. Have another student pour the dyed water into the oil. Wait a moment to watch the two separate and explain to the students that this was how many people thought the Jews and Gentiles should be, in the days before Peter's dream. They thought that the two groups should remain separate, because they had different beliefs about what they should eat and how they should worship.
4. Set out another clear container and have a student fill it with a cup (8 liquid ounces) of warm water (not boiling, but warmer than room temperature). Have another student add ½ teaspoon salt to the water, and stir or shake until the salt and water combine.

5 Say to the students, "This is why Peter had his dream: To show that all peoples are to join together, and not to be separate. The Gospel was intended for all of them, and the Good News is for all of us today, too."

Coloring Page

A Vision of Animals

Peter had a kind of dream where God told him to eat foods he wasn't supposed to eat. It showed him that God has erased the old lines between Jews and Gentiles. Gentiles can come into God's people now too, because neither they, nor pigs and shrimp, are unclean. God has made it *all* clean.

Acts 10:1-48
A Vision of Animals: God is Doing Something New

Lesson 19: What Do Gentiles Have to Do to Be Saved?

Food Activity

God's Family Is For Everyone

Materials

- 1 set of chopsticks for each student
- 1 small plate for each student
- 1 small bag of gummy candy, allergen-free and age-appropriate
- 1 small bag of mini marshmallows and another of raisins or small dried fruit
- A few marbles of varying sizes, if used for older students where it would not be a choking hazard. Otherwise, cereal such as Cheerios may be used.

Directions

1 Remind the students of what the lesson emphasized. Say, "In our lesson, we learned that some people thought only God's special people, the Jews, were allowed to believe in Jesus. But when those who weren't Jewish started to believe, some of the Jews were concerned and insisted that, in order to follow Jesus, those new believers had to practice the same laws and rules that Jewish people had followed for many, many years. That's why it was so important for the apostles to remind everyone that the Gospel was for all people, and that, 'Keeping the law does not save people. People are saved by the grace of Jesus Christ, who came and kept the law perfectly, even though no one else can do that.'"

2 Have students sit in a circle, and pass out a set of chopsticks and a small plate to each student. Give the first student a small piece of gummy candy, such as a Lifesaver or gummy worm. Have the student grasp the candy with the chopstick and pass it to the next child's plate. That child should then repeat the action and pass to the next until the candy makes it around the circle. You can then give each child a piece of that candy to eat (be careful to choose an allergen-free candy that is recommended for your class's age range).

3 Repeat the same cycle with items that are increasingly difficult to grasp, such as a mini marshmallow, a piece of dried fruit such as a raisin, and then end with a marble, the most difficult of all. **Note: Do not use marbles for younger children, as they are a choking hazard. You can substitute a Cheerio here.**

4 Ask the students how they would feel using chopsticks for every meal, if they had grown up using forks and spoons. Tell them that, in many cultures around the world, chopsticks are used for meals. Remind them that this is known as a cultural difference and is just something new and different for them, exactly as the things the Jewish people practiced were culturally different for the Gentiles.

5 Remind them that the lesson teaches us that the Gospel is for everyone and that, "Cultural differences are not wrong, as long as the most important thing is treated as most important: that Jesus is the son of the One True God, that he died, was buried, and rose again, and that he invites everyone to join his family."

Coloring Page

Christians Around the World

Christians from different countries all pray and sing about God, but they all do it in different ways. And that is OK! God made all kinds of people, and these kinds of differences are not a bad thing. Here we see a church service in Ghana (a country in Africa) and a church service in Canada (a country in North America). They look very different, but in both places the people are celebrating who Jesus is and learning how to live as his followers.

Acts 15:1-35
Christians Around the World

Lesson 20: Salvation By Faith

Craft Activity

Why Do We Need the Law?

Materials

- Two sheets of plain white paper for each student, each sheet cut into a square (you can use a standard sheet of printer paper cut just enough to become a square)

Directions

1. Today's lesson was about the law God had given his people. Remind the students of the law's purpose: "In his letter to the Romans, the Apostle Paul says that it is impossible for anyone to keep God's law perfectly. Instead, God's law is something like this: Imagine asking a group of people to draw as straight a line as possible without a ruler or a straight-edge, such as a hardcover book or a box. You might be able to draw a line that looks quite straight. But when you put your line next to the ruler or straight-edge, you see that it is not quite as straight as you thought. It dips and buckles here and there. That's what God's law does, Paul says: it shows us how far we are from perfect, even if, by our own lights, we seem pretty close to perfect."
2. Have the students give examples of things that are hard to do without a guide. Prompt them if necessary (fixing a car, computer coding, surgery, putting together a complicated toy, etc.). Say, "Today, we are going to try something two ways. First, we will try it without instructions, and then we will attempt it again with the directions and see which way goes better."
3. Give each student a piece of paper. Explain to them that they will practice "origami," which is the Japanese art of taking paper and folding it into shapes that resemble animals or flowers or other items. You may want to show them photos of examples. Say, "Now, without any instruction from me, please take your paper and fold it into the shape of an insect." Tell them they can only make the shape by folding the paper, not by rolling or twisting it.
4. Give the students a few minutes to attempt the bug shape. If they become frustrated, remind them that it's ok. It may also be helpful for them to see you attempting it as well! They'll get to try again with help. Once everyone has completed their bug shapes, say, "Most of us cannot make bug shapes without guidance. This is what our lesson taught us about the law: It is like a set of instructions, giving us guidance for how to live."

5 Now, give each student a fresh piece of paper, cut into a square shape. Follow the steps below (images are included) to create an origami insect:

- Fold the paper in half diagonally, so that it is a triangle.
- Fold the bottom two corners over so that they touch the top corner, creating a diamond shape. Then, fold the two flaps created in this step down and at an angle so that they form the wings of the bug.
- Take the top of the shape and fold the top piece of paper over so that the corner just touches the base of the wings. Then fold the bottom piece of paper over so that it is partially covering the previous fold made in this step.
- Now take the sides of the shape and fold them underneath the bug to finish shaping it. Finally, fold the corners of the "head" in to give the insect a pointed shape.

6 Once each student has finished, remind them of this important truth from the lesson: "The instructions helped us, just as the law helped God's people. However, '. . . perfect law-keeping isn't the way that we are made righteous before God. Rather, we are made righteous by *believing* in God.' The law is useful, just as our instructions were useful, but believing in God is the most important thing of all."

Coloring Page

Abraham

Abraham wasn't considered righteous because of rule-following, but because he listened to what God told him and believed it, even when it was difficult.

Romans 3:21-31, Romans 4
Abraham's Faith

Lesson 21: Essential Love

Demonstration

Can You See God's Love In Me?

Materials

- 2 cups red cabbage (must be red/purple color)
- Pot large enough to hold cabbage and water to cover it OR strong blender (there are two methods available to use, in case a stovetop is not available)
- Enough water to cover cabbage in pot or blender
- 3 clear glass or plastic containers (approximately 1-2 cup capacity each)
- 2 teaspoons baking soda
- A few tablespoons filtered water
- A few tablespoons lemon juice
- Pre-printed pH indicator (can be found online), printed in color to demonstrate acids and bases

Directions

1. Gather students in a group and say: "Do you remember the story the author mentioned at the beginning of today's lesson? She talked about how her son loved to test items to see what they are made of. She also talked about how doctors can use tests to see if we are sick. Today, we are going to make our own tests!"
2. You will be creating a testing fluid to check for acids or bases in today's activity. Since using boiling water around children can be tricky to manage, we recommend that you use the blender method or prepare the cabbage solution in boiling water ahead of time. If you choose the latter, bring additional cabbage to show them what you used to create the fluid. Explain that red cabbage contains something called flavin. Tell the students that scientists need to know if items are either acids, neutrals, or bases. This is called the pH of the item. The flavin in the cabbage will turn either red (for acids), purple (for neutral items), or green (for bases).
3. To prepare the fluid ahead of time, simply place 2 cups of cabbage in a pot, cover with water, and boil for 10-15 minutes, or until you can see that the water has turned color. Cool and then pour cabbage/water mixture through a strainer, reserving the colored water. This will be your testing fluid.

4 To prepare in class, put cabbage in a blender and cover with hot water. Do not allow the students to use the blender! Once the water has turned color, strain the mixture.
5 While allowing water to cool, show the students the pre-printed pH scale and say, "Now we will test 3 items. The cabbage water will change color depending upon what type of item we have." Note: There are incorrectly-colored pH scales on the internet, so make sure you choose one that shows red as acid, purple as neutral, green/yellow as base.
6 Divide the cabbage water equally into three clear containers. In one, add filtered/bottled water. The color should change slightly to blue/purple. Compare against pH chart, showing that the water is neutral.
7 Repeat with another container, but add lemon juice. The color should change to dark red, indicating an acid. Repeat with final container, adding baking soda. The color should change to green/yellow, indicating a base.
8 Say to the students, "We can test these liquids to show what they are: Acids or neutrals or bases. In the same way, we learned today that there is a test to show whether or not we are followers of Jesus. It's not a test that can be conducted in a lab or an experiment. Instead, Jesus said the test is that we love each other. The more kind and loving we are to everyone, even those who are hard for us to love, the more we show Jesus's practices of kindness, caring, and compassion. It will be as beautiful to see as the colors we saw today."

Coloring Page

God is Love

If you say that you love God, but don't show love to other people, John says that you are not telling the truth. You are lying. Jesus shows us what God's love—**true** love—looks like. Jesus came to earth, giving up all his privileges, and sacrificing himself to save us. That is what love is. It is self-sacrificing. It gives things up for other people. God does not leave us on our own to try to love people in this way. Rather, he has sent his Spirit to live in us to enable us to love one another as God has already loved us.

I John 4:7-21
God Is Love

Unit 7

The Life of the Church

Lesson 22: The Shared Life of Jesus' Followers

Food Activity

Let's Make a Meal!

Materials

- English muffins, already sliced in half (enough for each child to have a half; there may be some children with gluten intolerance, so a gluten-free option is a good idea to have on hand. If you cannot locate gluten-free English muffins, a corn tortilla is an alternative.)
- Marinara sauce (you'll need enough to put a tablespoon on each muffin half)
- Shredded mozzarella (¼ cup for each muffin half; if you have lactose intolerant students, have a lactose-free option for them as well)
- Sliced, cooked pepperoni pieces (¼ cup for each muffin half)
- Sliced olives
- Access to a microwave or oven
- Paper plates and napkins
- A piece of paper and a pencil or crayon for each student
- "My Pizza Order" page (Page 81)

Alternate option listed below in Step 5 if microwave or oven is not available.

Directions

1. Gather the students together and say, "In today's lesson, we learned about how generous the believers were with each other! They didn't just meet together on Sundays. They ate all of their meals together, and shared with each other, too, taking such good care of one another." Tell the students, "Today, we are going to practice that same generosity by making each other a meal."
2. Give each student a square of the "My Pizza Order Form," and break them up into groups of two, if possible. Have them write their partner's name on the top of the form and then say to their partner, "What would you like on your pizza today?" Next, they should check the box beside each item the person would like on his or her pizza.

3 Once their orders have been taken, each student should be given the supplies to create their partner's pizza (after washing their hands!).
4 Help the students assemble the pizzas and take turns microwaving them just until the cheese melts. If there is an oven available, that can be used by the teacher only.
5 **If there is no access to a microwave or oven of any kind, an alternative activity would be to have each child place a cupcake or cookie order. You may have pre-baked cookies or cupcakes and let the child add the toppings or fillings (for cookie sandwiches) that their partner requests.**
6 Once the pizzas are ready, let them cool for a moment, and then allow the students to pass them out to their partners. Say, "Doesn't it make you feel good to give a meal to your friends? And doesn't it feel great to have someone make and share a meal with you? That is what the first Christians did, and that is what we can practice in our lives, too."

Coloring Page

Sharing What We Have

The first followers of Jesus shared what they had with each other.

Just like God helped them to do that, God is with us, and God's grace helps us to be generous, to be joyful, to share what we have, to help one another, to eat together, and to welcome others to join us.

My Pizza Order

❏ Pepperoni
❏ Extra Sauce
❏ Extra Cheese
❏ Olives

My Pizza Order

❏ Pepperoni
❏ Extra Sauce
❏ Extra Cheese
❏ Olives

My Pizza Order

❏ Pepperoni
❏ Extra Sauce
❏ Extra Cheese
❏ Olives

My Pizza Order

❏ Pepperoni
❏ Extra Sauce
❏ Extra Cheese
❏ Olives

My Pizza Order

❏ Pepperoni
❏ Extra Sauce
❏ Extra Cheese
❏ Olives

My Pizza Order

❏ Pepperoni
❏ Extra Sauce
❏ Extra Cheese
❏ Olives

Acts 2, 4, 5, and 6
Sharing What We Have

Lesson 23: Sharing Different Gifts Within the Community

Put It into Practice Activity

Using Our Gifts for Everyone's Good

Directions

Decide on a project you would like to complete with the class. It should be a communally beneficial project in which each child can contribute her "gift" in a practical way. See suggestions below for ideas, or make up your own. Once you pick a project, wrap each project item as a gift (use gift wrap, recycled paper, gift bags, whatever you wish to make it look like a gift) before the lesson time. Perhaps even give some thought as to which gift you will give each child, and label each gift with a name. After reading the lesson, tell the children you will be giving out gifts to use for a project you'll all do together today. You could explain the project before or after gifts are opened. Hand out gifts to each child, saying to each, "May you enjoy this gift and use it for the good of the people here today." You could make it even more ceremonial by having each child reply, "I will!" You could let the children open their gifts at the same time, or you could let them take turns so that everyone sees what "gift" each child has and will use (and you can offer any explanations or positive commentary on the spot if necessary).

Use these project suggestions as a starting place. Feel free to add, subtract, or change items for gifts. Thrift stores are wonderful places to find some of these items or whatever items you want to use.

Start a garden: seasonally-appropriate seeds, old spoons, potting soil, egg cartons or toilet paper/paper towel rolls or newspaper (for making seed starter cups), old plastic/paper cups or small spray bottle for watering, tray for holding the seed starter cups

Cook mini-pizzas: sliced bread/English muffins or tortillas or pita pockets, grated cheese, chopped fresh tomatoes/peppers/mushrooms/olives/onions/pineapple/pepperoni/ham, small cans of tomato paste, oregano (chopped fresh food items can be packed into separate sturdy ziploc-like bags)

Bake and decorate cookies: premade cookie dough, candy decorations, chocolate chips, sprinkles, small bowls of colored sugar (mix granulated sugar with inexpensive liquid food coloring), colorful mini-marshmallows, premade frosting (if using already-baked cookies)

Create dinner table decorations: paper or cloth napkins (beforehand, you could cut squares from an old cotton sheet or piece of clothing and hem the four sides of each square for napkins), cardstock or unused file folders (from which to make placecards and centerpieces), colorful paper scraps, glue stick or bottle of white glue, colorful markers, small scraps of fabric or yarn, glitter, toilet paper/paper towel rolls (for napkin rings)

Clean a communal household appliance: rubber gloves, small carton of baking soda, small bottle of white vinegar, small spray bottles (in which to mix water and baking soda or or water and vinegar), squares cut from old clean flannel sheets or clothing (to use as cleaning cloths), surface to clean such as a deep freezer/refrigerator/stove/dishwasher/kitchen sink, batch of cookies, sliced apples (for a work break!)

Decorate a part of the home or classroom: acrylic/craft/latex paints in small cans or bottles, inexpensive artist's paintbrushes in various sizes, stencils (can premake from old file folders or cardstock), dabbers such as erasers/corks/pieces of sponge, old plastic/paper cups to hold water and paints in, a primed surface to decorate (wall space, a door, an old or small piece of wooden furniture in good repair such as a stool/chair/bookcase/coffee table—maybe just put a big bow on this as a gift!)

Coloring Page

When Body Parts Argue

Body parts are supposed to work together. Just like it would be silly for parts of a body to argue with each other, members of Christ's body should try hard to work together peacefully, and with love, instead of arguing and competing over who is most important.

I Corinthians 12, Romans 12
When Different Parts of the Body Argue

Lesson 24: Don't Be Divided

Group Game

Working Together Works Better!

For this activity, you will be playing a game that demonstrates how the body of Christ should work together as one. The first round of the game is similar to a normal game of Sardines. This is a game much like traditional hide-and-seek, except only one person hides, and everyone else tries to find him or her.

1 For the first round, everyone will be working separately. Say to the students, "In today's lesson, we read about problems that kept happening in the days when the church was just beginning. We learned that some people did not want to work together like one body, where the arms and legs and feet and hands and heart all functioned together as they should. Instead, we saw that people kept breaking off into little groups or trying to be separate from the rest of the church or body. Today, we are going to play a game, but we will play it in two different ways. One time, each of us will just work on our own, without helping anyone else. The next time, we will work together as a team. Let's see how much faster and better things can go when we care for and help each other."

2 Select one student to be "it." Give them a set amount of time to hide while the other students are closing their eyes (the amount of time will be determined by the size of the playing area). Once time is called, the students split up and search for "it." Each time someone finds the hiding spot, he or she joins "it" in that spot. This continues until the last person has found the group. Remind the students that they are NOT to help each other. They are to try to remain as quiet and still as possible once they locate "it," so as not to let on where the hiding place is. Time the group to see how long this round takes.

3 Next, gather the students together and let them know how long it took for everyone to find "it." Tell them that they are going to play the same game again but, this time, they will work as a body instead of competing against each other. When one person finds "it," he or she will call out to the rest of the group and lead them to the hiding location as well. Time the group to see how long this round takes.

4 Once the game is finished, gather the students together and discuss how each round went. Say, "Working together does not mean everything will go perfectly. Some people might have fallen down, or some might have been confused by the rules. Working together DOES mean that we all know we are important to the group, and we all have something to share, whether it is the ability to find someone or to help someone up or to

make sure we all find the right spot. It can sometimes make the job easier and sometimes make it more fun, too, and most of all, it shows everyone that we believe in the value of each person in the body."

Coloring Page

God Makes the Church Grow; We All Get to Help

Paul says that we should think about the people who teach about Jesus as we might think of gardeners. Some people plant the seed by telling others about Jesus. Others water the seed and take care of it by continuing to teach them about Jesus, and by sharing the good life of the church with them. But if anyone believes in Jesus and continues to grow in faith, it is because God makes them grow—just as it is only God who can make a plant grow, even if we plant the seeds and take care of them carefully.

I Corinthians
God Makes the Church Grow; We All Get to Help

Lesson 25: What is Faith, and Why Do We Suffer?

Demonstration

Faith and What We Cannot See

Materials

- Lemon juice (either fresh or from a container is fine; you'll just need enough for each student to have approximately one tablespoon of juice)
- Small cup for each student
- A piece of paper for each student
- One cotton swab or small watercolor brush per student
- Heat/light source: You may use an incandescent light bulb or a lit candle, both of which will require adult supervision

Directions

(Note: Since the lemon juice needs to dry completely, it may be best to do the activity before the lesson.)

1. Say to the students, "In today's lesson, we heard about people who lived and acted in faith. What does that mean?" Give students a chance to answer, and then make sure to follow up their answers by replying, "The idea of faith is that we are acting on something we cannot see. We trust and believe that certain things will happen, even though we can't see them yet."
2. Tell the students, "Today, we are going to practice making something that requires faith. We will be writing something down, and then it will disappear! We won't be able to see it! But we trust that it is still there."
3. Give each student a piece of paper, a cup with one tablespoon of lemon juice in it, and a cotton swab or paintbrush. Tell them to use the lemon juice to write a secret message on the paper. They need to use enough juice to dampen the paper but not soak it.
4. Allow the papers to dry completely, and then have an adult help with the next step. Holding the paper over either a light bulb or a lit candle will reveal the message. Just be

careful not to hold the paper so closely to the light source that it catches fire! Have the students read their now-visible messages aloud.

5 Say, "Even when you could no longer see your message, you knew it was there. That's just like faith: We believe in what we cannot see. Even when things are not clear to us, we can trust and have faith that God is still working."

Coloring Page

People Who Showed Their Faith

This lesson talks about people who trusted in God, even when everything around them made their faith seem strange or even ridiculous: Noah built an ark because God told him to do it. His neighbors laughed at him and thought he was crazy, but he did it because of his faith, because God had promised that the ark would save him and his family. Abraham left his home to move far away to a place where he knew no one, because God told him to, and promised to make Abraham's family into a great nation—even though Abraham and his wife, Sarah, were old and hadn't had any children. Abraham went because he had faith. Moses gave up his comfortable life as a prince in Egypt to lead God's people through the wilderness, because he had faith in God.

Hebrews 11
People Who Showed Their Faith

Lesson 26: Faith Must Express Itself in Works, Not Just Words

Group Game

Making Our Words And Actions Match

Materials

For this activity, you will be setting up an obstacle course that will be maneuvered blindfolded. It does not need to be anything elaborate, so choose simple items. You can set up plastic buckets that the students need to walk around, hair brushes that they need to locate and pick up, empty soda bottles for them to locate, or mop handles for them to walk alongside. The important thing is to avoid items with hard edges (blocks or bricks) that would be painful to walk into.

You will also need two blindfolds.

Directions

1. Have the obstacle course already set up. Here are some suggested objectives for the course:
   - Set up plastic buckets in a line that the student will have to weave around.
   - Lay a hairbrush on the ground that the student will have to locate and pick up.
   - Set soda bottles in various rows, so that the student will have to locate them and line them up in another row.
   - Put a broom or mop handle on the ground and have the student find it and then walk parallel to its end.
2. Divide the group into two teams. From each team, choose one Obstacle Course Caller and one Obstacle Course Walker. Blindfold the walkers and have those students sit out of earshot of the rest of the group. Tell the rest of the group, "In today's lesson, we learned that our words and our actions need to match up. This means that, if we call ourselves followers of Jesus and we say things that don't help people, or we say one thing but do another, our faith is empty. It doesn't work! Today, we will do an experiment to show what happens when words and actions don't match."
3. Whisper to the group that the point of the game is for the Obstacle Course Walker to make it to the end of the course before the walker from the other team does. Except

there's one tiny twist! The Obstacle Course Caller will say the OPPOSITE of what the walker needs to hear. In other words, if the soda bottle that needs to be picked up is on the walker's right, the caller will say, "Go to your left!" If the bucket is in front of them, the caller will say, "Step around the thing that's behind you!" Tell the class, "Let's see what happens when our words don't match what our actions should be!"

4 Bring the blindfolded students back into the room and set the callers up at the end of the course. Have them begin calling out instructions, and if they get stuck, suggest some to them, reminding them (without the blindfolded student hearing) that they have to give the opposite directions.

5 Once the blindfolded students have attempted the course for several minutes, they will probably begin to be frustrated, so don't let it go on for too long! Have them remove their blindfolds, and reveal to them the twist of the game.

6 End the activity by saying, "Just like our lesson showed us today, our words and our actions need to match. We saw what happens when they don't! If we say we love Jesus, our actions need to show that. If we are supposed to take care of those who don't have enough food or clothing, then we should take actions that help them, not that harm or discourage or ignore them."

Coloring Page

Love in Actions, Not Just Words

The children say they love their dog. But they never remember to keep his water bowl full. When their mother asks them to take the dog for a walk, or throw the ball for him, they groan and roll their eyes. The children's "love" for the dog doesn't mean much if they don't take actually help to take care of the dog. Just like that, if we say we love Jesus, we should show it by doing things that help other people.

James 2
Love in Actions, Not Just Words

Unit 8

After Death

Lesson 27: Peter Heals Aeneas and Raises Tabitha

Group Game

Believing the Unbelievable

Directions

1 Today's lesson is about miracles. Ask the students what they think the word "miracle" means. After they give their definitions, explain the reason for miracles, according to the lesson: "*Jesus said that his disciples (now apostles) would perform miracles and wonders in his name so that people would believe, and that is what happens here.*" Miracles were special, because they were incredible things that occurred so that people would believe in the power of Jesus, the one the apostles were teaching and preaching about.

2 The activity for today is a game based upon "Two Truths and a Lie." In this game, each student will take turns sharing three stories. The person who shares comes up with two things about him or herself that are true—for example, a student could say: *1. My favorite animal is a dog, 2. I once broke a whole tooth on some hard candy, and 3. I ate six pieces of pizza at one time.* Only one of these "facts" is not true. The game is more interesting if the truths are stories that seem unbelievable! The teacher can start with a personal example and should encourage the students to try to share facts that the rest of the group would not already know about them. Once a student has shared, the class votes on which of the three statements is the lie (have them vote for 1, 2, or 3). Then the student reveals the actual answer. Give each student a turn to participate.

3 Tell the students, "Miracles are events that seem unbelievable and unexplainable, just like some of your stories today! But as we learned in our lesson, 'Luke tells us that the miracle of Dorcas being raised from the dead became known all over the land, and that more and more people came to believe in Jesus. That is why miracles are important. They get people's attention and surprise people. They help people to believe and to hope in the final resurrection and restoration of everything in the entire world.' "

Coloring Page

Peter Brings a Woman Back to Life

This woman, Dorcas, used to make clothes for poor people. When she suddenly died of an illness, Peter brought her back to life.

Acts 9:32-43

Peter Brings a Woman Back to Life

Lesson 28: Suffering, Then Glory

Review Activity

Is Anything Able to Separate Us From God's Love? NO!

Materials

- Nothing Can Separate Us From God's Love (Page 101), one copy for each student
- Pencil for each student

Directions

1. Give each student a copy of the word search entitled "Nothing Can Separate Us From God's Love" (Page 101)
2. Say to the students: "Romans 8:35-39 asks us to consider various things that we sometimes *think* can separate us from God and His love. It reminds us, however, that none of these things has that ability. You will find these things listed below in the word search list. They may be vertical, horizontal, or diagonal. They may be written forward or backward. As you complete the word search, ask yourself about each word: Can *this* separate me from God? No. Can *this*? No! What about *this*? No!!"
3. If the students need help, use the answer key below to help them.

		H										H				N
		A											T			A
	T	R	O	U	B	L	E							A		K
		D													E	E
E		S							R							D
R		H		S						E						N
U		I			L						G		E			E
T		P	E	R	S	E	C	U	T	I	O	N				S
U			O	W		P	G				I		A			S
F			O	W	R			N		M				D		
		R		E	E				A				E	E		
	D		S			R	E	F	I	L		P		M		
		E					S				T			O		
	N				T	H	G	I	E	H				N		
T														S		

Coloring Page

Patiently Waiting Through the Pain

Sometimes a doctor or dentist might have to do things that hurt, but it is because they are making broken parts of us better again. Just like that, we sometimes go through hard times, but we know that after the pain, things will be better. We know this because Jesus defeated death and returned to life again, and is working to make everything right.

Nothing Can Separate Us From God's Love

X	Y	H	T	E	S	K	A	S	R	A	P	H	I	P	H	N
Z	L	A	F	E	P	H	E	C	B	F	P	I	T	O	H	A
E	T	R	O	U	B	L	E	Z	A	V	K	C	X	A	O	K
A	A	D	P	O	O	D	V	I	N	N	G	U	Z	Z	E	E
E	R	S	A	E	M	J	A	R	R	D	L	M	G	H	J	D
R	S	H	B	S	D	X	O	M	C	E	N	I	W	A	K	N
U	F	I	Q	U	L	P	O	R	P	X	G	L	E	Y	W	E
T	H	P	E	R	S	E	C	U	T	I	O	N	E	L	L	S
U	P	V	O	W	U	P	G	O	H	W	I	B	A	K	U	S
F	J	I	O	W	R	L	V	N	I	M	T	K	U	D	B	O
R	T	R	F	E	E	N	Q	Y	A	F	C	H	E	E	S	E
E	D	A	S	L	U	R	E	F	I	L	O	P	H	M	E	O
S	J	E	N	B	E	D	S	E	A	N	T	H	C	O	F	D
C	N	J	O	O	T	H	G	I	E	H	J	I	G	N	J	H
T	A	Y	C	Z	S	H	O	K	X	R	F	Y	T	S	E	H

trouble
nakedness
life
future
hardship
danger
angels
powers
persecution
sword
demons
height
famine
death
present
depth

Romans 8:18-39
Patiently Waiting Through the Pain

Lesson 29: Living Between the Times

Group Game

Keep Going!

Materials

- One deck of Uno cards

Directions

1 Tell the students, "In today's lesson, we learned about hope. How do we keep going even when things are hard? Remember that we read about the church in Thessalonica, how the Holy Spirit and the way the believers loved and cared for each other helped them keep believing and keep moving forward, even when setbacks or persecution or sadness came to them."

2 Ask the students to raise their hands and give examples of setbacks or hard things they or people they know have experienced. Then say, "We are going to play a game that helps us practice how to keep going even when events or situations make it seem like we are going back."

3 This game is called "Red Card / Green Card." To play it, you will need a deck of Uno cards. It is similar to a game of Red Light/Green Light, but the Uno cards are drawn to determine the movement. The class stands in a horizontal line with the teacher standing across the room from them. To begin, the teacher draws a card for the whole class and everyone takes the same step (the cards and their corresponding meanings are listed below). After the first movement, the teacher draws one card for each student and shows them the color, reminding them of what type of step they will need to take. If the teacher makes it all the way through the deck before the game is completed, he or she may reshuffle and start over. The game ends when all of the students reach the finish line (where the teacher is standing). However, in order to demonstrate how important it is to help each other during setbacks, any student who reaches the end may then go back and stand with another student who is still attempting to reach the finish line. Tell the students, "Sometimes we can do things to help those who are going through hard times, and sometimes we can just stand beside them so that they know they are not alone."

4 Once all students have reached the finish line, remind them of this statement from today's lesson: ". . . to hope in the Resurrection, to have faith in God, and to love one

another in this world where so many bad things happen is not always easy. That is why Paul prays for the churches, and asks God to help them. If we believe in Jesus, we can have faith that God will help us to love one another and live well and to keep hoping for God to make everything right even when things look bad . . . This is what makes Christians hopeful even when things around them are bad."

Uno Card Instructions:

A. Green number cards mean one big step forward.
B. Yellow cards mean one small step forward.
C. Red cards mean one step back.
D. Blue cards mean one hop forward.
E. Draw Two cards are two small steps forward.
F. Draw Four cards are two small steps forward and the student immediately gets another turn. However, he or she may give the turn away to another student before seeing what movement the card indicates.
G. Skip means the student does not move on that turn.
H. Reverse means that the student takes two small steps back.
I. Wild card means that the student picks between two other random cards.

Coloring Page

A Church Gathering in Thessalonica

This small group of people is the church in Thessalonica that Paul wrote his letters of Thessalonians to. They met each week in someone's home to pray, sing, eat together, and learn about Jesus.

1st Thessalonians
A Church Gathering in Thessalonica

Lesson 30: The Importance of the Resurrection

Review Activity

Analogies for Understanding

Materials

- Analogy Cards (Page 108) *(Optional: print them on cardstock)*
- scissors
- pencil and paper
- chalk and chalkboard, OR whiteboard or easel (with paper) and marker
- dictionary(ies), science dictionary, biology dictionary, or any age-appropriate books about living things
- encyclopedia set or online encyclopedia
- online search engine

Option 1:

1. Print and cut out the Analogy Cards (Page 108) and have them ready for students before class. You should have two piles of cards; one with the ". . . as (noun) is/are to . . .)" phrases and the other with the ". . . (noun)." words.
2. Write the following sentence on the chalkboard/whiteboard/easel paper: "**Resurrection is to Christianity as feathers are to birds.**" Below it, write, "Resurrection is to Christianity as . . ."
3. Pointing to the sentence, say to the students, "We learned in the lesson that resurrection is to Christianity as feathers are to birds. This type of comparison, which shows a relationship, is called an analogy. The particular analogy in this lesson demonstrated a relationship of *uniqueness* (being one-of-a-kind) so that we could understand how important resurrection is. Today we will match some phrases to some words, from the world of animals and plants, to create additional analogies that show other relationships of *uniqueness* that will give us further understanding."
4. Spread the cards out on a table, but keep the two piles separate from each other. You could mix the two piles together if you think the students are up for the challenge.

5 Now tell them that they should match the phrase cards to the word cards. Tell them they can use any of the reference materials you've provided to learn definitions of unfamiliar words and to answer two helpful questions: "What one characteristic is unique to the (noun from word card)?" and "What animal or plant grouping has the unique characteristic on the phrase card?" Give them all help needed with this research and then finding the unique relationship. This should be fun and not frustrating. For example, if research starts to stall, look information up yourself and show them where to read.
6 When they've correctly matched all cards, have various children read aloud each analogy while you write them on the chalkboard/whiteboard/easel paper, starting with, "Resurrection is to Christianity . . .", then (phrase from phrase card) (word from word card). (to see the pattern, refer to the bolded analogy sentence from Step 2)
7 If there is time and interest, let students comment on their new understandings, especially as they relate to resurrection and Christianity.

Option 2 (more challenging):
Similar to Option 1, but make photocopies and provide a set of cards for each student. After each student correctly matches the cards, have them each write down the analogies on paper.

Solutions:

- as milk is to mammals
- as backbones are to vertebrates
- as a set of eight legs is to spiders
- as honeymaking is to bees
- as meat is to carnivores
- as plants are to herbivores
- as a singular muscular foot is to molluscs
- as exoskeletons are to arthropods
- as ringed segments are to annelids
- as water vascular systems are to echinoderms
- as spiny coverings are to echinoderms
- as flowers and fruits are to angiosperms
- as ingestion (eating for energy) is to animals
- as photosynthesis (converting light to food) is to plants
- as woody trunk tissue is to trees
- as xylem and phloem are to vascular plants

Coloring Page

Jesus is Alive Again!

Jesus appeared alive after his death and burial to many people, including a group of more than five hundred men and women. One day, God will raise us back to life just like he did for Jesus.

...as milk is to...	...mammals.
...as backbones are to...	...vertebrates.
...as a set of eight legs is to...	...spiders.
...as honeymaking is to...	...bees.
...as meat is to...	...carnivores.
...as plants are to...	...herbivores.
...as a singular muscular foot is to...	...molluscs.
...as exoskeletons are to...	...arthropods.
...as ringed segments are to...	...annelids.
...as water vascular systems are to...	...echinoderms.
...as spiny coverings are to...	...echinoderms.
...as flowers and fruits are to...	...angiosperms.
...as ingestion (eating for energy) is to...	...animals.
...as photosynthesis is to...	...plants.
...as woody trunk tissue is to...	...trees.
...as xylem and phloem are to...	...vascular plants.

1st Corinthians 15
Jesus is Alive Again!

Unit 9

Last Things

Lesson 31: Christ, the Mighty Conquering One

Craft

Jesus Holds the Keys

Materials

- One key for each student
- Nail polish in various colors
- Nail polish remover
- Sharpie markers in various colors
- Small star stickers
- Floral wire
- Smock or old shirt for each student

Directions

1. Begin by saying to the students, "Wasn't that a powerful image of Jesus that we read about today?" Read some of the words that the lesson used to describe Jesus (powerful, strong, triumphant, gentle, brings peace) and ask the students how thinking of Jesus in those terms makes them feel.
2. Re-read the verses from the lesson to them: "Do not be afraid," Jesus says to John. "I am the First and the Last. I am the Living One; I was dead, and now look, I am alive for ever and ever! And I hold the keys of death and Hades (the grave)." Say, "In this description of Jesus, we see Him as someone who holds the keys to death, something that is very powerful. But He is more powerful than even death! Today, we are going to make our own keys to remind us of this image of Jesus."
3. Make sure that each student has a smock or old shirt to protect his or her clothing, and spread out newspapers or paper towels to protect all surfaces.
4. Give each student an old key, and show them how to paint it with nail polish. Encourage them to use a thin coat so the paint will dry faster! You may also use the hair dryer to speed up the process or, alternatively, have them paint the keys before you read the lesson so that there is more drying time.

5. Once the key is dry, allow the student to use markers to decorate the key. He or she can write a word on there that reminds him or her of the Jesus they learned about today. They can also use the star stickers to decorate the key, or can draw stars on by hand, to remind them of the verse describing Jesus as standing among the stars.
6. After each key is decorated, cut a small length of floral wire (3-4 inches) and thread through the hole at the top of the key, twisting to secure. This allows the student to hang the key somewhere.
7. Say, "When you are afraid, you can look at this reminder that Jesus is more powerful than any force on earth, and that he is the bringer of peace to each of us."

Coloring Page

Jesus the King

In the book of Revelation, John had a vision of Jesus as powerful and kingly. In this vision, Jesus stands among the lamps that represent the churches. Jesus is with us and is powerful enough to fix what has gone wrong in the world.

Revelation 1
Jesus the King

Lesson 32: God Makes All Things New

Craft Activity

Making Things New

Materials

- Sturdy paper plates (not styrofoam, but not thin paper plates; one for each student)
- Gold glitter glue or gold glitter and glue to mix together
- Scissors for each student
- Markers

Directions

1 Begin by recapping the lesson: "That last part of our lesson is an important, beautiful thought. We read this . . ."

> We can see clearly what it is that Christians hope for. We hope for the final defeat of death. We hope for the ending of pain and suffering and tears. We hope to be with God forever and ever. This is how God always wanted it to be. And this is how it will be one day.

2 Ask the students to think for a moment about things that might fall under the categories of "pain" or "suffering." If age-appropriate, they might share examples, but only if they volunteer to do so. Say, "As Christians, we have the hope that one day, all things will be made new. It doesn't mean that the hard, bad things didn't happen, but that God will make the world the way it was meant to be, before suffering and sadness came into it."

3 Explain to the students that you will be making an example of *kintsugi* today. This is an art form from Japan where something beautiful comes out of something that seems to be broken. When a plate or bowl or cup breaks, the cracked pieces are put back together, with gold filling each crack. Not only is the piece useful again, it is more beautiful than ever. The cracks have become art. You may also want to show them images from a Google search of the word *kintsugi*.

4 Give each student a paper plate. Have them write "God will make all things new" on it, using a marker. Then, have them cut the place into a few pieces, no more than four. Finally, give them gold glitter glue and have them put a generous amount along each crack, enough that it will dry golden.

5 Conclude by telling the students, "We are not saying that we are glad the bad things happen. We are just remembering that, as Christians, we hold onto the hope that God can heal us and show us beauty even when sad and hard times happen."

Coloring Page

A New World

In the final chapters of the Bible, we see God's plan for the conclusion of the story. The language that John uses in the book of Revelation is like poetry. It doesn't tell us *exactly* how everything will be, but it gives us a good idea. God will be with us. God will wipe away our tears. And in this new city that God will build for us, to live among us, there will be no more death, no more crying, no more pain—just the way God always wanted it to be.

Revelation 21
A New World

Lesson 33: Come, Lord Jesus

Food Activity

God's HospitaliTEA

Materials

- herbal tea bags—use a variety made from leaves such as mint, lemon balm, passionflower, or raspberry. Or, include just one variety made from leaves, and use other flavors the students might like, such as chamomile or rose hip
- a variety of cut-up and colorful fruit such as pineapple, mango, banana, apples, melon, or anything native to your area (include berries, if you want)
- toothpicks for students to pick up fruit pieces
- attractive trays on which to arrange the fruit
- mugs with sturdy, wide bases (to prevent getting knocked over)
- pan or kettle in which to boil water (or, insulated containers in which to store previously boiled water or pre-steeped tea)
- ice cubes
- jugs of cold water (clear jugs would enhance the image of thirst-quenching water)
- table around which everyone can sit and see each other

Directions

1. Prepare and lay out everything in advance so that the set-up table is ready for students to enjoy.
2. As part of this preparation, decide how you want to prepare the tea.
   a. You can have pre-boiled water in insulated containers (or kettle or pan), let each student choose a tea bag, and pour the water into the mug. If you do this, be sure to do the pouring and steeping away from the students to prevent burns and to allow the tea to cool down. Use ice cubes to cool the tea faster, if you want.
   b. You can pre-steep different flavors of tea and store them in insulated containers.
   c. You can pre-steep different flavors of iced herbal tea and serve it from jugs (again, clear jugs enhance the differing colors of tea). Steep tea for five minutes for strength, let it cool, then pour into ice-filled jugs.
3. Invite students to "God's HospitaliTEA" table.

4 Give each student a tea bag that has leaves in it, and tell them to open up the bags and examine the leaves (see, smell, feel, listen).
5 Say, "In the verses we read from the Book of Revelation, John describes God's hospitality and welcome to us. He mentions thirst-quenching water and abundant fruit on the tree of life. He also mentions that the leaves of the tree of life are for healing. Are you enjoying using your senses to examine the tea leaves? In a minute, you'll get to use your sense of taste when we drink some herbal tea. For many people, enjoying a cup of herbal tea IS healing and relaxing. Let's enjoy some tea, cold water, and fruit together; and be refreshed by this tiny glimpse of God's hospitality and welcome towards us!"

Options:

- Create a card, naming the event "God's HospitaliTEA," to put in the middle of the table.
- Put a potted plant and/or a vase of flowers on the table to represent the restored earth, and mention this connection to today's lesson.

Coloring Page

The River and the Tree of Life

John saw a vision of how the world will be one day: God is there, with his people, there is abundant fruit on the tree of life, and there is a river flowing through the city to quench the thirst of anyone who wishes to come. "Let the one who is thirsty come; and let the one who wishes take the free gift of the water of life." This is not a God who is eager to cast people out. This is a God who loves to welcome people.

Revelation 22
The River and the Tree of Life

Unit 10

These Three Remain: Faith, Hope, and Love

Lesson 34: Faith

Group Game

What We Can Count On

Materials

- place markers (coins, candies, or pebbles)
- game die (one for each game board)
- tokens (small candies or coins or marbles)
- copy of What We Can Count On game board (Page 123) for each group of students playing together
- set of Cards (Page 124) for each game board

Directions

1. Read, "Psalm 74:16-17 tells us this about God: 'The day is yours, and yours also the night; you established the sun and moon. It was you who set all the boundaries of the earth; you made both summer and winter.' God has made certain things about His creation that are reliable. Imagine what it will be like when we finally see God make a new world with no more death! Until then, we practice faith about that."
2. Game play: each student takes a turn by rolling the die and moving his/her marker forward the number of spaces indicated by the die. When he/she lands on a "Take a card" space, he/she reads a card and answers the question. For each correct answer (all answers should be "yes"), the player collects a token. For each incorrect answer, go back one space. If you need to adjust the questions to suit your region, do so. If players run out of cards before the end of the game, reshuffle them and use them again. *(Option: the opposing player can make up new questions for the person to answer.)* At the end of the game, players get to keep their tokens.
3. When students are done playing, ask them to tell you what practical things they can do to practice their faith that God will make all things well in the end. Some ideas in case they need prompting might be: memorize the Lord's Prayer, recite some other memorized passages such as Romans 8:35-39, read some uplifting Psalms aloud, practice some mindfulness exercises (search "mindfulness exercises for kids" on the internet for a plethora of ideas), do something kind for someone in need, talk with a trusted adult if troubled about

something, think about what you might like to do as an adult and research your ideas, sit outside and stare at nature around you for thirty minutes.

Coloring Page

Faith

Today's coloring page is a verse about faith. Faith means holding onto believing in Jesus, and continuing to live in a way that shows we believe in Jesus, even when things are difficult.

What We Can Count On

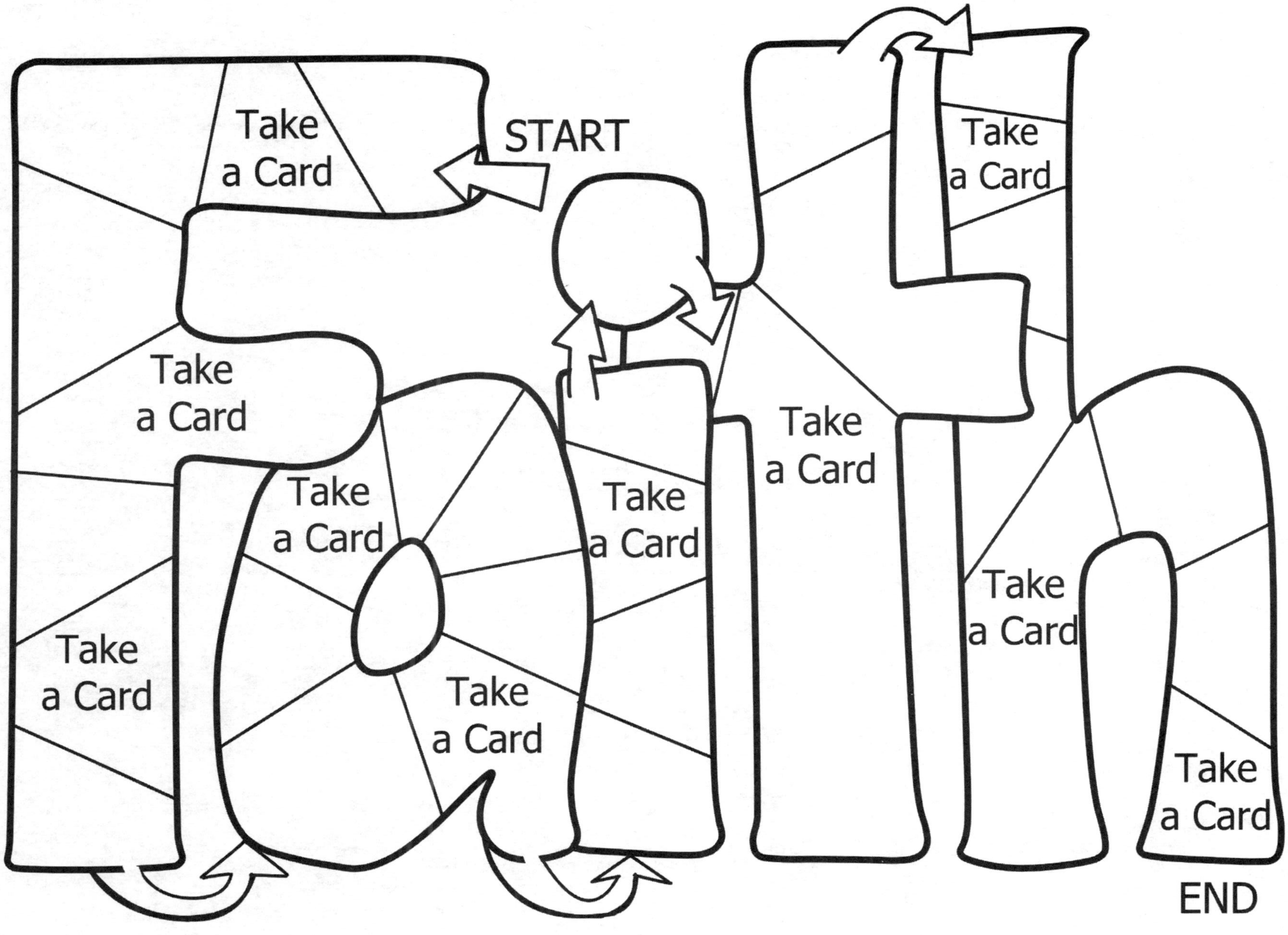

Does the sun rise daily, even when clouds fill the sky?	Did you experience any warmth outside during the last summer you experienced?
Does gravity normally keep us stuck to the earth (not counting people who are launched by space ships!)?	Is your heart muscle still beating without you squeezing it?
Does water quench thirst?	Did flowers bloom during the last spring you experienced?
Are your lungs still inflating today without you squeezing air into them?	Does the sun set every evening, even when we can't see it?
Does a square have four corners?	When you went outside during the last winter, did you experience air that was cooler than the previous summer?
Will the moon show itself to be full every month?	Do the trees in your area bud leaves every year?
Did trees shed their leaves during the last autumn you experienced?	Do the the constellations Big Dipper (northern hemisphere) or Southern Cross (southern hemisphere) appear in the sky every year?
Did plants of any kind grow in your area in the past year?	Will a well-constructed and sturdy chair hold you up while you're sitting in it?

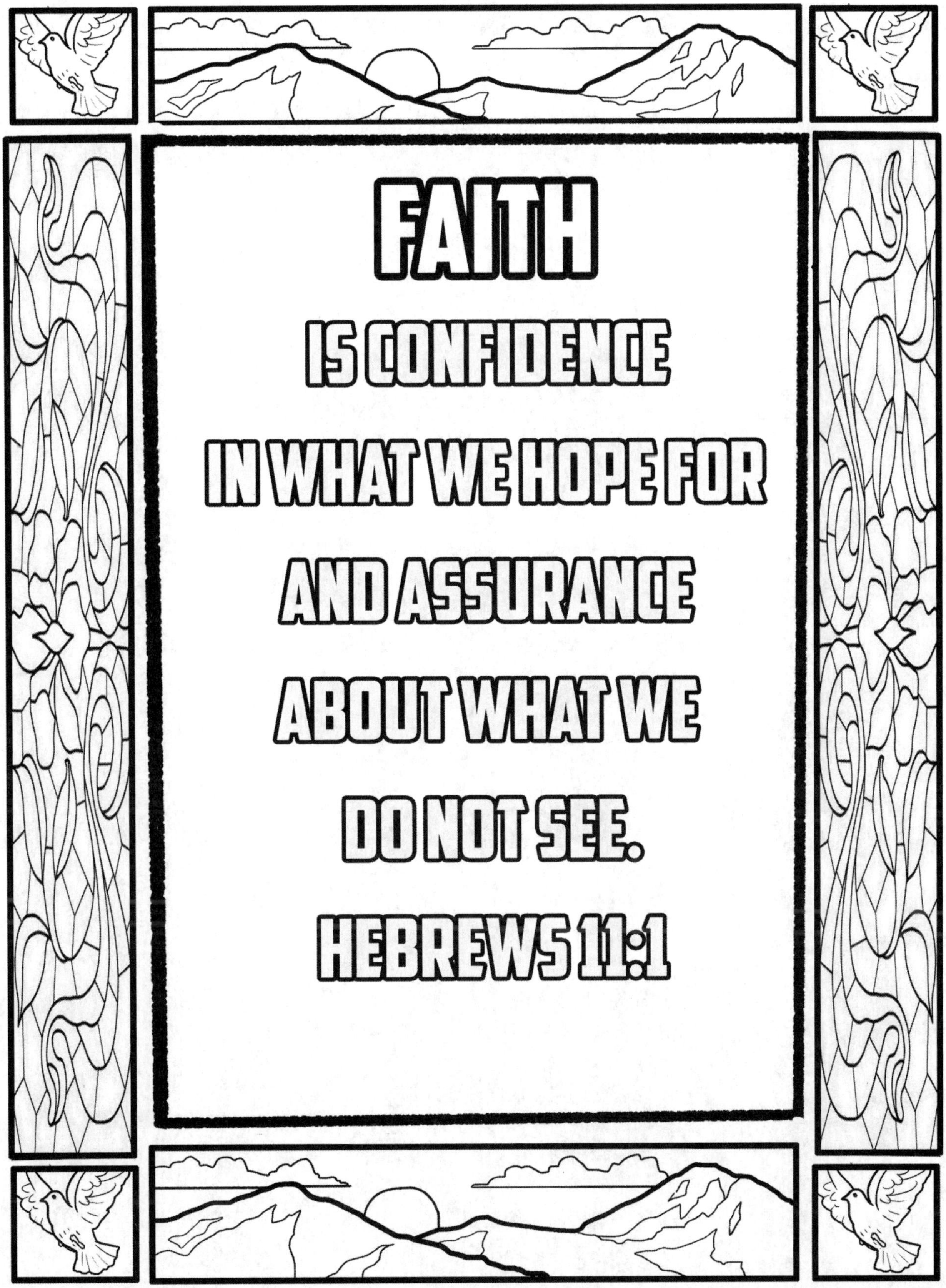

Hebrews 11, Ephesians 2:8-10, and James 2:22
Faith

Lesson 35: Hope

Memory Work

A Famous Poem About Hope

Materials

- glue sticks
- pairs of scissors
- colorful poster board, one piece (approximately 9" x 12") per student
- copies of the mixed up lines of the poem, one per student (Page 129)
- a copy of Emily Dickinson's poem " 'Hope' is the Thing with Feathers" for each group of students to refer to (Page 128)
- markers, crayons, and/or colored pencils

Directions

1. Say to the students, "We learned that hope means knowing that God has already taken care of the end, no matter how things are going. Around one hundred sixty years ago, a poet named Emily Dickinson wrote a poem called ' "Hope" is the Thing with Feathers.' The first stanza (first four lines) in particular give us a great way to picture hope inside us, where it never stops singing a tune to us. Today we'll create posters of this poem after I read it aloud to you."
2. Read the poem aloud, being sure to take your time. Explain the unfamiliar words and phrases before or after you read the poem aloud the first time: "Gale" is a strong wind, "sore" means extreme or severe, "in extremity" means in extreme or severe situations.
3. Then lead the students in a second reading.
4. Have the students cut their copies of the mixed up lines of the poem. The black lines surrounding each poem line are cutting guides. Each poem line should then be a separate piece of paper.
5. Letting them refer to their group copies of the poem, have them reassemble their cut lines into the proper order. Once the lines are in order, students can lay them out on the poster board in order and glue them down (9 inches is the width and 12 inches is the length).
6. They can then use the art supplies to illustrate their posters. Suggest that they think of ways to illustrate the first stanza in particular, because it is so visual.

7 End with some questions for students to answer: "What is hope?" "It's the thing with feathers!" "Where does hope perch or rest?" "It perches in our souls!" "Does it ever stop singing its wordless tune to us?" "No!" "How long can we hope in God?" "Always!"

Option:

- When posters are completed, try having everyone read the poem together from their posters. Lead them in this reading, and take your time.

Coloring Page

Waiting in Hope

This girl is waiting for the sun to rise. She is eagerly waiting for it, confident that it will happen, even though it hasn't happened yet. That is what hope is like. We believe that God will make everything right, because he started making things right by sending Jesus to us.

Hope is the Thing with Feathers
By Emily Dickinson

"Hope" is the thing with feathers -
That perches in the soul -
And sings the tune without the words -
And never stops - at all -

And sweetest - in the Gale - is heard -
And sore must be the storm -
That could abash the little Bird
That kept so many warm -

I've heard it in the chillest land -
And on the strangest Sea -
Yet - never - in Extremity,
It asked a crumb - of me.

And sweetest - in the Gale - is heard -
And on the strangest Sea -
That could abash the little Bird
That perches in the soul -
That kept so many warm -
Yet - never - in Extremity,
And never stops - at all -
It asked a crumb - of me.
"Hope" is the thing with feathers -
I've heard it in the chillest land -
And sore must be the storm -
And sings the tune
without the words -

Romans 8, Romans 15, 1st Peter 3:15
Waiting in Hope

Lesson 36: The Greatest of These is Love

Review Activity

What Is God's Love Like?

Materials

- pencils
- markers, crayons, or colored pencils; in case students want to decorate their papers
- copies of the student page "What Is God's Love Like?" (Page 132), one copy per student
- supplies for a celebration! It's the end of the year; do what you want! Make it simple with heart-shaped cookies and a drink, or go all out.

Directions

1. Hand out the writing implements and student pages to students. Give any help needed with reading the Bible passage aloud. *Option: Have everyone read it aloud together.*
2. When everyone is done filling in the blanks, it's time to celebrate! Eat and talk and play together.
3. During the celebration, encourage students to find ways to practice some of the things that love is: being patient, being kind, protecting, not envying, not being rude.

Coloring Page

The Greatest Gift

Love for other people—showing care for them with our words and actions—is better than anything else. It's what God wants for us, because it is what God is like.

What Is God's Love Like?

Read this aloud by yourself or with a partner (take your time so you can read clearly):

"First Corinthians chapter 13, verses 4 to 7 and verse 13. Love is patient, love is kind. It does not envy, it does not boast, it is not proud. It is not rude, it is not self-seeking, it is not easily angered, it keeps no record of wrongs. Love does not delight in evil but rejoices with the truth. It always protects, always trusts, always hopes, always perseveres...And now these three things remain: faith, hope, and love. But the greatest of these is love."

Now fill in the blanks with words or phrases from the text:

1 Corinthians 13:4-7 Love is ____________________, love is ____________________. It does not ____________________, it does not ____________________, it is not ____________________. It is not ____________________, it is not ______________________________, it is not easily ____________________, it keeps no ____________________. Love does not ____________________ but rejoices ____________________. It always ____________________, always ____________________, always ____________________, always ____________________. 1Corinthians 13:13 And now these three remain: ____________________, ____________________, and ____________________. But the ____________________ of these is ____________________.

1 Corinthians 13:13; and 1 John 4:8-16
Love is the Greatest Gift